Vij's Indian

Our Stories, Spices, and
Cherished Recipes

Vij's Indian

Our Stories, Spices, and
Cherished Recipes

Meeru Dhalwala   Vikram Vij

PENGUIN

an imprint of Penguin Canada Books Inc., a division of Penguin Random House Canada Limited

Published by the Penguin Group
Penguin Canada Books Inc., 320 Front Street West, Suite 1400, Toronto, Ontario M5V 3B6, Canada

Penguin Group (USA) LLC, 375 Hudson Street, New York, New York 10014, U.S.A.
Penguin Books Ltd, 80 Strand, London WC2R 0RL, England
Penguin Ireland, 25 St Stephen's Green, Dublin 2, Ireland (a division of Penguin Books Ltd)
Penguin Group (Australia), 707 Collins Street, Melbourne, Victoria 3008, Australia
Penguin Books India Pvt Ltd, 11 Community Centre, Panchsheel Park, New Delhi – 110 017, India
Penguin Group (NZ), 67 Apollo Drive, Rosedale, Auckland 0632, New Zealand
Penguin Books (South Africa) (Pty) Ltd, 24 Sturdee Avenue, Rosebank, Johannesburg 2196, South Africa
Penguin Books Ltd, Registered Offices: 80 Strand, London WC2R 0RL, England

First published 2016

2 3 4 5 6 7 8 9 10

Photography by John Sherlock

Artwork for section openers and cover are details taken from a 30' wide by 9' high painting in My Shanti Restaurant dining room produced in the Mithila or Madhubani Art tradition by Indian-based artist Kamlesho Roy.

Thanks to Paris Forrer for her assistance with the food photography. And, thanks to Sital Dale for preparing every recipe with Meeru and simultaneously writing each one in Punjabi while Meeru wrote in English.

Printed and bound in China

LIBRARY AND ARCHIVES CANADA CATALOGUING IN PUBLICATION

Dhalwala, Meeru, author
Vij's Indian : our stories, spices and cherished recipes / Meeru Dhalwala
and Vikram Vij.

Includes index.
ISBN 978-0-14-319422-4 (paperback)

1. Cooking, Indic. 2. Cookbooks. I. Vij, Vikram, 1964-, author
II. Title.

TX724.5.I4D44 2016   641.5954   C2016-902154-8

eBook ISBN 978-0-14-319423-1

www.penguinrandomhouse.ca

COOKING IS THE DOORWAY TO
CARING ABOUT WHERE OUR FOOD COMES FROM,
TAKING CARE OF OUR FAMILIES AND
TAKING CARE OF OUR HEALTH.
IT CONNECTS OUR HANDS TO OUR SENSES AND
TO EVERYONE'S HEARTS.

THIS COOKBOOK is dedicated to Ritu Dhalwala, a full-time working mom who cooks out of necessity but who believes in food's ability to connect people and nourish our bodies and minds. More importantly, this book is dedicated to Ritu's "Mommy Soup," a quick and healthy dinner of canned chickpeas or kidney beans, chopped bell peppers and sautéed garlic with turmeric and salt that's eaten with brown rice … and spicy pickles for adults. It has sustained her twins, Raiya and Miles, and her husband, Gregg, for years, and her children love it more than any other meal.

At big family gatherings, there will always be Mommy Soup somewhere next to all of the meat and vegetable curries and salads. And our daughters, Nanaki and Shanik, gladly help themselves to large servings of their aunt's soup.

Through the years, we have seen Ritu turn many of our recipes into variations of Mommy Soup during the week, and Gregg on weekends recreate many of them as they are meant to be prepared. However you make them, we hope that you enjoy our recipes as they fit into your lives, with a mixture of necessity and beauty.

CONTENTS

INTRODUCTION

Each of our cookbooks is a personal journal of notable events related to eating and recipes. The recipes we feature are both the dishes we eat at home and the meals we create at the restaurants. At times our home and our restaurant families get blurred, but for us, that abundance of love and community is the beauty in our lives. In fact, it's our lifeline. The difficulty is that these personal and professional lives can interfere with one another, and neither Vikram nor Meeru wants to draw lines of distinction between them.

In *Vij's at Home—Relax, Honey*, we recounted the story of our daughter Shanik coming home from elementary school and announcing she was angry at her mother for never having given her Cool Whip. Shanik wanted to eat Cool Whip like the other kids, not the fresh cream that we whisked and served instead. Shanik's announcement was a reminder to this restaurant family that our kids want to be "in the know" about the yummy foods other kids eat in public without losing the Indian, or "special," foods we eat at home. Our daughters do not want to be known as "foodie" kids.

At the time that *Vij's at Home* was published, in 2010, Nanaki and Shanik were fourteen and eleven years old. Vikram and Meeru had been running Vij's restaurant for sixteen years and Rangoli for about eight. Our routine was normal yet specific to our own family and work.

Meeru would wake up very quietly. First thing in the morning she doesn't enjoy anyone or anything but her coffee and her reading of various journals on food and environmental issues (she officially put this reading in her job description). She mustered up a good-morning smile and made breakfast for everyone, part of her work as a member of the "family team." Her quiet joy officially started when the house emptied out by 8 am. An hour or two later she was running in her neighbourhood, contemplating what she had just read and what she was about to cook that day. She'd return from her run, finish up her computer work and, by noon, she'd be in her Vij's or Rangoli kitchens. For the rest of the day and into the night she became a social butterfly with her small and intimate groups of people.

Vikram, however, would wake up talking. When it was his turn to make breakfast, he'd get up early to serve Nanaki, Shanik and Meeru, his favourite customers, even if all three of us were morning cranks. When Nanaki said, "What I want for breakfast, Papa, is no talking at the table," he treated the comment as if his favourite customer was not happy and he set about making her happy. By 8 am, Vikram was on his cellphone, most likely talking to someone in Toronto, and on his way to work. Vikram loves his loud meetings, but then—and still now—he'd take a break to talk to customers having lunch at Rangoli, go back to his cellphone and meetings, and then crash for his forty-five-minute nap. He is quiet and non-social only when he is sleeping. Or doing yoga, which he resurrected from his childhood days in India as an attempt to calm down his body and mind. At 4 pm our family gathered for coffee and something sweet, and by 5:30 Vikram was on the floor of one of our restaurants, hosting customers.

As our girls grew older and each of us became more successful, we began talking about expanding our businesses. Both of us wanted to expand in different ways: Meeru had small-scale ideas, whereas Vikram felt strongly that the time to go big with food production was now or never. Vikram also had a love of food television and wanted to be a part of it, while Meeru watched little television, period.

Our differences got the better of us, and 2011 turned into a tumultuous year. We were married business partners and parents who'd been Velcroed to each other twenty-four hours a day for seventeen years. Up until that time, Nanaki and Shanik, as well as our staff, only knew "parents" who argued yet always made up in front of them. The making up had always, at an emotional level, been comforting for the girls (not to mention the staff!). Suddenly, though, there was hardly any making up, and new arguments were layered on top of unresolved old ones. Nanaki started to take Shanik ice-skating on Saturday and Sunday afternoons because it was unbearable to witness Mama-Papa screaming and yelling at one another with no filters on.

By October we realized that we were becoming different people with different interests and life experiences, and that each of us was becoming unaccepting of the other. We were frustrated that our professional ties were as important as, and intertwined with, our personal ties. At work, Meeru would go from laughing to quietly scowling when Vikram walked into the kitchen. At the same time, Vikram didn't bother saying hello to anyone in the kitchen because he didn't want to talk to Meeru, with whom he had just finished arguing at home. One day, even though no words had yet been exchanged, Amarjeet Gill, our general manager and head cook for our kitchens, started crying. She claimed that we had no right to spread our negativity into "her kitchen of happy sisters."

We were stuck, yet afraid of change. How do you change a relationship without losing its built-up love? How do you prevent that love from being torn apart by relatively recent disagreements that are quickly turning into vitriolic resentment? How do you change a relationship that involves two children whose lives you do not want to disrupt—children whose lives are already being disrupted by bursts of very loud, angry arguments between their parents? At the same time that we were trying to deal with marriage and kids, we had over a hundred employees: Vikram was managing the front of house, and Meeru, the kitchens. The Vij-Dhalwala answer was to cook dinner, both separately and together, and always for the family. The best and wisest money we ever spent together was to renovate our home kitchen into our dream cooking space.

On Saturdays, Nanaki and Shanik would return from ice-skating around six o'clock, when they knew that Meeru would be cooking a big dinner, once again relaxed and in her Zen place. On Sundays, the girls knew that, by six, Mama and Papa would have put any argument on hold because nothing would—or could—ruin a nice bottle of wine and a Sunday night dinner. Cooking dinner was the precious line both Vikram and Meeru knew never to cross. Why? Because cooking transforms us from whatever storm we're in the middle of back to a calm security. The act of cooking is the one thing we do not fail at, even if our meal isn't the best tasting on a particular night.

Although we each felt the other was going to ruin the chance to accomplish what we wanted individually, we knew that neither one of us could succeed without the other, no matter what. We were even more tied to each other professionally than parentally. Meeru suggested counselling; Vikram said communication was not the problem—we already knew too much of what the other was thinking. Meeru suggested that maybe counselling would both give us filters and organize our communication; Vikram said the lack of filters was our beauty and he didn't have the wherewithal to learn a new form of communication, as if it were a new foreign language being introduced on top of everything else. We were unravelling as a couple, but not because of a lack of communication. We were unravelling because we were sick of being in one another's personal and professional space all the time.

One thing Meeru and Vikram have in common is an ability to make decisions very quickly and take action. We talked about marriage and were married one month later. We talked about expanding the original fourteen-seat Vij's restaurant and signed a lease for a bigger space two months later. We talked about having our first child, and Nanaki was born nine months later. This is one trait we share, and it drives many people around us crazy. Once we make a decision, we don't have the patience to wait for others to get on board. In November, we told the girls that Vikram was moving into his own apartment but that we were going to remain a family. This did not go over well.

"Why are you both so weird?" asked Nanaki, then fifteen. "Why can't you do anything like normal parents? Why can't you just say you're splitting up instead of pretending you're not?"

Shanik, aged twelve, added: "Mom, you tricked me, and I'm really mad! All this time I've been helping you cook dinner, doing the dishes and cleaning up the kitchen, and you said that these weren't chores but were part of my teamwork for the family. And now my family just broke up and I wasn't even part of the team to decide this. My family just broke up and I had no say in it. You and Papa are an unfair team."

We had this conversation with the girls over a dinner of pork chops, roasted potatoes, sprouted mung bean and carrot salad, and leftover chickpea curry. Nanaki was biting into her pork angrily with big tears rolling down her face. Shanik, though showing her anger at her mother with flared nostrils, was leaving Vikram's part of the meal untouched; she ate only the chickpeas and salad. (Meeru is almost certain that Shanik developed her maniacal love of chickpeas and sprouted mung beans that evening. While we are not proud of how she came to love these two healthy foods, we're relieved that she finally got over pasta and cheese.) The more we said that we weren't getting a divorce and that this was just a way for us to get along better, be better parents and work together, the more angry the girls became. Like the Cool Whip situation, they wanted to be normal children of normal, separated parents. They didn't want the foodie version of marital separation.

On January 1, 2012, Vikram took some bedding and boxes of clothes to his new apartment. At noon he phoned and asked if we were still going to have lunch together, as usual, and Meeru yelled at him, "No!" But by 4 pm, he was back home for afternoon coffee, and was still there for Sunday night dinner. We just did what came naturally. We were both ashamed and stung by Shanik's comments that we took away her power as a team member where it mattered the most for her. We were embarrassed by Nanaki's comment that we were weird. We wanted and needed to get to work on creating a new normalcy as quickly as possible, and dinner was the easiest normal for us.

For that January first dinner we made *rajma chawal* (kidney beans and rice), a comfort food that is the equivalent of macaroni and cheese and that we eat once a week. Vikram cooked the Basmati rice, and Meeru made the kidney bean curry. For all of Vikram's celebratory robustness with food, he has inherited from his mother the patient and delicate hand required to make perfect Basmati. That evening we were all feeling so raw and sensitive that Meeru used canned kidney beans, since the noise of our pressure cooker releasing steam while cooking dried beans would have shaken us up. Meeru cut up carrots and celery and tossed them with a bit of lemon, salt and black pepper for her crunchy side dish, and Vikram ate *ghatia*, crunchy chips made with deep-fried chickpea flour, as his side. The girls just enjoyed the dish with no crunch and picked out the small bits of ginger.

Without ever discussing the logistics, the four of us continued on with everything that we did together. The big difference was that Meeru and Vikram quickly created a new respect for one another, since we had previously run it to the ground. With our own physical spaces, we had a break from each other and were sincerely happy to see one another at work every day. We have become an even stronger, more united professional and parental team than we were before. We divide our work properly. We discuss our projects with one another during the day instead of when we are tired and irritated at 11 pm.

Within a few months, we'd found our new groove. Vikram lived in what he called his "dwelling," but all of us shared one family home. The girls got to stay at home, and the fact that Vikram and Meeru stopped fighting made everything that much easier. Meeru kept ghatia in the cupboard at all times. The pressure cooker went back on.

Almost a year later, in November 2012, we opened Shanik restaurant in Seattle (which we closed in March 2015). Meeru oversaw the Seattle operations, since she is American. She rented an apartment there and, for the first time, spent three months away from Vancouver. Vikram would live in the family house for those three months and, for the first time, would be the sole, full-time parent. While Meeru was turning into a bundle of nerves, Vikram couldn't keep the smile off his face.

A few days after Meeru reached Seattle, she had a phone call from Nanaki. "Mom, I don't think Papa understands that he has to actually go to the store and buy food. There's nothing in the fridge and there are no apples. We ran out of all the groceries you bought before you left." Meeru pretended to be concerned, but she was smiling that they missed her grocery shopping. She called Vikram.

The next day, Nanaki phoned again, in a panic. "Mom, Papa bought the wrong apples. Even though we told him we like Fuji, he bought the Gala kind and he bought ten of them and they're gonna get all mushy. I don't think he knows how to buy fruits and vegetables. And he also didn't buy the Avalon organic milk with the cream on top. He bought regular milk." Meeru phoned Vikram again. We talked groceries for a minute and work support for an hour.

Shanik

Nanaki

A few days later, after Vikram was buying the right apples and organic milk, Shanik called. "Mom, Papa is feeding us too much meat. Can you call him and tell him not to? He won't listen to me."

Our family's comfort level had returned. We had managed to figure out how to be a family in our food- and restaurant-obsessed world. Whether we are labelled separated, business partners or Mama-Papa, we are a team. The girls have adapted too, as we all do. In our family, the food that best tells this story is ginger.

In the 1970s, when Meeru and Vikram were growing up, ginger was the spice that everyone's mother added to Indian food. Meeru's parents had recently moved to the United States, and though Meeru's mother, Omi, felt extremely isolated in a new country where she didn't speak the language, where her classical singing and fashion sense weren't appreciated and where she didn't like the processed foods her kids kept asking her to buy, she threw herself into cooking. She bought produce at the local farmers' markets and Underwood Deviled Ham, Dinty Moore stews, Chef Boyardee spaghetti and meatballs, and Froot Loops at the grocery stores. Meeru's parents hated the taste of these prepared foods—especially the combination of canned meats and mayonnaise— but as long as their daughters were hungry for their nightly vegetarian Indian dinners made with whole-wheat chapattis, they could "munch" away. Omi reserved the word "eating" for their Indian food.

Raised to believe, like all Indians, that ginger and turmeric were keys to good health, Omi snuck these spices into every non-Indian food (except the Froot Loops!). Of course, Meeru and her sister, Ritu, didn't like ginger even in their Indian food and asked their mother to stop using it. Instead, Omi chopped the ginger as finely as possible to make it "invisible." And though Omi insisted that there was no ginger in their food, she yelled at her daughters when she caught them meticulously spitting out each tiny piece. If Omi didn't yell at them for spitting out the ginger, the girls knew their mother was preoccupied with her loneliness. Getting in trouble for spitting out ginger came to mean that all was normal at home. In Vikram's home, his mother added ginger to everything in huge chunks, no hiding. Luckily, Vikram loved ginger even as a child. In fact, the ginger and tamarind candies were his favourites.

As an adult, Meeru has become a ginger (and turmeric) fiend and is almost as adamant about its nutritional and healing values as her mom was when she was a kid. Vikram, too, copies his mother's use of ginger and puts big chunks of it in his cooking. And like their mother before them, Nanaki and Shanik have long picked out the ginger and put it aside on their plate. Nothing irritates them more than when Meeru professes to cook a non-Indian recipe from a cookbook and adds ginger and turmeric to it! But this is starting to change.

Our first cookbook was a journal of our restaurant life and recipes. Our second cookbook was a journal of our home life and recipes. This third book is a journal of recipes that often blur the distinction between work and home and are cooked at both places. At home we just take shortcuts, ad libbing according to what's in the fridge and how much time we have to cook. We hope that you become comfortable enough with our recipes that you can improvise as well.

These are also recipes that result from life changes that happen to many families but are nevertheless special to each one. Nanaki moved to Montreal to attend McGill University. There, with her limited income and small kitchen, she mostly cooks variations of kale, chickpea and sprouted lentil recipes. She doesn't add ginger, but she loves turmeric and garlic. She doesn't cook meat in her dorm but she savours it when she comes home for visits. Meanwhile, Meeru, Vikram and Shanik continue on with their Sunday night dinners in Vancouver … and Shanik has blossomed into a ginger lover.

This is a cookbook for Indian home cooking, which is the source of our nourishment and health. We eat and enjoy meat, but at home we (especially Meeru) emphasize healthy, delicious vegetarian food, with a fun bonus of meat curries once or at most twice a week. The key to eating vegetarian meals is to make them so delicious that you don't even think of the meat. This is the beauty of Indian spicing. Over the past few years, Meeru's mother has suffered a series of strokes and she is now deaf and living with aphasia, which leaves her unable to speak, read or write. In January 2015, Omi spent a special month with Meeru to officially pass down the recipes that she has been cooking for her children, sons-in-law, grandchildren and many, many friends. Of course, many of these recipes feature ginger and turmeric. Turmeric is the anchor to Indian cuisine, so be sure to include it if it's called for. Ginger can be optional in most curries, but we encourage you to use it—either invisible or visible. You or the kids may spit it out for a while; however, like most Indians, there's a good chance you will end up loving it.

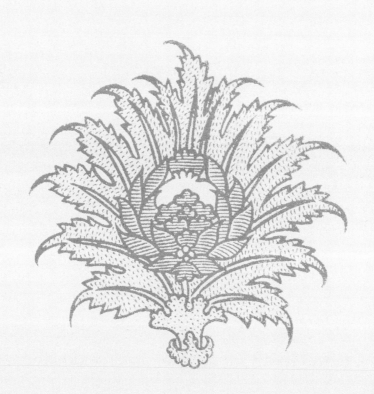

IN THE KITCHEN

INDIAN SPICES

In our two previous cookbooks, we have written copious amounts about spices—everything from what plants they come from to what medicinal benefits they have. Our goal in this book is to keep things simple, to make Indian cooking seem as familiar as making lasagna. You don't need a cupboard full of spices until you know that you'll be cooking Indian food fairly regularly. The ones you will need to have on hand are turmeric, cumin (both seeds and ground) and ground coriander. If you leave out all the other spices in these recipes and just cook with these three, you'll still have a nice curry.

We haven't outlined all the medicinal benefits of our spices here, but it's important to note that in Indian culture, we eat not only to enjoy the taste of foods but also to bring health to our bodies. Well-digested meals result in healthy bodies, which by nature prevent illness. Without a peaceful and clean inner body, we can't achieve the energy balance inside and out that's needed for spiritual peace of mind. And yes, oil and salt play a big role in helping the spices taste great for body and soul!

While we roast and grind our spices (for health and freshness) and highly recommend it, it's not necessary. You can buy your spices in ground form. We do recommend, though, that you roast your own cumin and coriander seeds for better flavour. And if you do cook Indian food regularly, it's worth investing in a designated coffee grinder just for your spices.

AJWAIN SEEDS These tiny and strongly flavoured seeds are sometimes called Indian thyme. If you use too much of them, you'll get a bitter taste. We also use ajwain as a hot herbal tea to prevent sinus colds and to help digest our food when we've eaten too much. One teaspoon in 6 cups of water is more than enough.

ANCHO CHILI POWDER We use mild ancho chili powder in our recipes. This Mexican chili complements Indian spices with a hint of smokiness but without the heat. Ancho is the (red) dried form of (green) poblano peppers. Previously, we used Mexican chili powder, which is often a combination of ancho and other types of chilies along with salt, but we now prefer pure ancho chili powder in our curries. If you can't find ancho, go with Mexican, but remember that it may taste slightly different.

ASAFOETIDA This spice is the resinous gum from an herbal plant. In North America it comes in powder form and is mixed with a bit of flour to keep it from getting sticky. The first thing you will notice about asafoetida is its smell—not nice. Once you cook it in oil, though, it becomes mild. You need very, very little (¼ teaspoon per six or so servings) and it is by no means necessary, but it does add an indescribable and subliminal layer of spicing, especially to vegetarian dishes.

CARDAMOM, BLACK These brown pods contain moist black seeds. We peel off the pods, discard any dry seeds and use only the moist seeds in cooking. Dark brown or black seeds are moist and flavourful, and these are the ones we use. If the seeds are very dry or light brown, they will not taste good at all. The reality is that in a pack of black cardamom pods, you sometimes end up throwing away as many as a quarter of the seeds. That's because you can't tell until you open the pods whether the seeds are moist or dry. Black cardamom has a smoky, earthy flavour and is a crucial component of our Garam Masala (page 23).

CARDAMOM, GREEN Just like black cardamom, the darker the seeds, the fresher the taste. Green cardamom has a sweet and floral flavour, and we use it mainly for our chai and for desserts. Whole green cardamom pods—with the seeds—are also a natural breath freshener after a heavy meal full of onions and garlic. Just place one in your mouth and chew it slowly.

CAYENNE PEPPER In this book, we use dried crushed or ground red cayenne chilies to add heat to our recipes. Although we add cayenne to just about everything, it is optional if you're not a fan of heat. We add whole red chilies to our Lemon Pickle (page 29), but even those are optional.

CINNAMON We usually use highly aromatic cinnamon sticks in our curries, but we do grind them for our Garam Masala (page 23) and a few other recipes. If your sticks don't have a strong cinnamon smell, you won't get the cinnamon flavour in your curries.

CLOVES Like cinnamon, we use highly aromatic whole cloves in our curries and grind them for our Garam Masala (page 23). Be careful not to use too many of them, or you'll get a bitter taste. You can add five or six cloves to *any* Basmati rice pilaf. Although we sometimes take the whole cloves out of our dishes before serving, mostly we leave them in and let our guests know they're there.

CORIANDER SEEDS These seeds from the cilantro plant have a mild lemony and floral aroma. Do not let this fool you, though—too much coriander can ruin your curries. For this book, you will need ground coriander seeds, and the finer you grind them, the stronger the taste. We grind the coriander seeds to the texture of freshly ground black pepper. Ground coriander goes stale faster than other spices, and for this reason we do not add it to our Garam Masala (page 23). We add it separately to our curries.

At home, we roast 2 cups of coriander seeds in a frying pan on medium-high heat for 3 to 5 minutes, or until the seeds give off an aroma and turn a few shades darker (some of the edges will turn very dark). We cool the seeds completely and store them in an airtight container. We grind a few tablespoons at a time and store the ground coriander in an airtight container as well. Roasted seeds will keep for up to 6 months. Ground coriander will keep at peak freshness for 1 month but will still taste good for up to 3 months.

CUMIN SEEDS These very hearty seeds can be used copiously. Cumin seeds have a milder flavour in cooking than ground cumin, and we use whole or ground cumin in most of our curries. Ground cumin is a key component of our Garam Masala (page 23).

At home, we roast 2 cups of cumin seeds in a frying pan on medium-high heat for 3 to 5 minutes, or until the seeds turn a few shades darker. Once the roasted seeds have cooled completely, we grind them all and store them in an airtight container in the dark. Ground roasted cumin will keep for up to 6 months.

When cooking with cumin seeds, we still roast them even though we will be cooking/sizzling them in oil. This step is not necessary, but it gives the cumin seeds better flavour. As a guide, the darker you can get your seeds when sizzling (but not black!), the stronger their flavour.

CURRY LEAVES Good fresh curry leaves have a deep green colour similar to fresh bay leaves. They are fragrant, and if you rub your hands through a stem of curry leaves, their "curry" aroma will linger on your fingers. Cook with them as you would with bay leaves and then remove them before serving your dish. Fresh curry leaves are hard to find in North America, except at Indian grocery stores, but if you can get them, add them to any onion or garlic when sautéing or to soupy curries when you add the water. We do not used packaged dried curry leaves because we find they have a stale flavour.

FENNEL SEEDS We use fennel seeds in a few of our curries and always in our chai. For chai, we do not roast the seeds. For curries, we roast the amount required in a small frying pan on high heat for 1 minute, or until the seeds turn a shade darker. (Since we don't cook with fennel seeds that often, there's no point roasting more than required.) Like green cardamom, fennel seeds are also eaten as an after-meal breath freshener and as a digestive aid.

FENUGREEK LEAVES Dried green fenugreek leaves, *kasuri methi*, give a wonderful added layer to Indian spicing, especially if you are cooking with cream. They add a flavour similar to a very earthy celery. Fresh fenugreek leaves are very different and are used as a vegetable, not a spice, so it's important not to confuse the two. Fresh fenugreek leaves are referred to simply as *methi*, while dried leaves are referred to as *kasuri methi*. In addition, do not confuse dried green fenugreek leaves with yellow fenugreek seeds!

FENUGREEK SEEDS Whole yellow fenugreek seeds are very bitter if you bite into them, so we always grind them for cooking. Their flavour is a combination of slightly tart and slightly earthy. After turmeric, cumin and coriander, we recommend that you add these ground seeds to your Indian spice cupboard. Fenugreek seeds will bring out the "curry" flavour in your cooking. This is the taste that many people associate with store-bought curry powders. Use ground fenugreek sparingly, as too much will make your curry bitter.

KALONJI SEEDS Also known as nigella, these beautiful small charcoal-coloured seeds add a toasted onion flavour to curries. Be sure to sizzle them in oil before adding them to any dish.

MANGO POWDER This powder is almost talcum-like in texture. It is ground from sun-dried unripe green mangoes. Mango powder, *amchur*, adds a mild, sweet and tangy flavour to curries. We also sprinkle it on fruit.

MUSTARD SEEDS These small seeds come in two colours: black and yellow. We mostly use black (and dark brown) mustard seeds in our recipes because they have a stronger flavour than the mild yellow ones. To ensure that they are cooked, mustard seeds must be fried (or sizzled) in oil for about a minute, or until they start popping. Raw or burned mustard seeds are bitter. We also use ground mustard seeds, which have a stronger, more tart flavour than the whole seeds.

PANCH PORAN This Bengali five-spice mixture consists of fenugreek seeds, kalonji seeds, fennel seeds, yellow or black mustard seeds, and cumin seeds. Panch poran is sold as premixed whole seeds, which we grind at home. This spice blend needs to be cooked in oil, otherwise you will have a raw-tasting, pungent curry.

SAFFRON These red threads from the crocus plant are expensive, but you get what you pay for. You need very little to give a curry or rice pilaf its elegant flavour, but cheap, low-quality orange or yellow saffron will provide no flavour at all. Be careful that you don't add too much saffron, as it will make your curry bitter when combined with other spices. Saffron will keep in a dark, airtight container for up to a month, but use it as soon as you can.

SALT, BLACK Black salt, *kala namak*, is actually pink and talcum-like in texture with a sulphuric smell. Once you mix black salt with other foods, its smell goes away and the mineral taste melts into the dish. For lack of a better explanation, black salt is to spices what cured anchovies are to fish. Black salt tastes particularly good on fruits such as apples, pears and bananas. And we think it's great in Yogurt (page 34).

STAR ANISE Although star anise is not usually thought of as an Indian spice, we like its pungent and slightly sweet licorice flavour. You can substitute star anise for cinnamon in curries (except our Garam Masala). Like cinnamon, if you can't smell the aroma of whole star anise, you won't get its flavour in your curries either. Avoid using more than necessary, as it will add a bitterness to your recipe. Use the spice whole, like cloves.

TURMERIC is the cornerstone of Indian cooking because it pairs with every other spice. Its earthy flavour is the basis of our curry, and it is the foundation of most of our Indian cooking.

For cooking, we use only turmeric that has been dried and ground. Fresh turmeric, which looks like orange ginger, tastes rough in a curry, although many Indians eat fresh turmeric mixed with a bit of lemon and salt as an Indian pickle. This is mostly for its medicinal benefits, as turmeric is an antioxidant, great for the skin and considered by most of us to help prevent cancer.

INDIAN STAPLE INGREDIENTS

As you'll see in our recipes, most Indian dishes are very forgiving. You can use whatever ingredients you have on hand, in different proportions, and you will still end up with a good-tasting meal. Here are a few staple foods that are used in many Indian dishes and that we often call for in this book.

BEANS are very popular in Indian cuisine, with kidney and garbanzo beans (chickpeas) being the most popular. In North America we also cook with navy, black and pinto beans. Indians are traditionally vegetarian, and beans are a great source of iron, protein and fibre. They are also filling and great for maintaining healthy blood pressure. There is a common belief in North America that beans give gas and should be avoided. However, releasing gas is not the problem: it's the associated smell. That unpleasant odour comes not from the beans themselves but from not chewing or digesting your food properly. To help with digestion, Indians add ginger to bean curries.

BREADS are served daily in India, usually as chapatti, which is a flatbread made from whole-wheat flour, all-purpose flour and bran. Making homemade chapattis is still very common in India, but they require time and lots of clean-up, which isn't always convenient with today's hectic schedules. Naan is a leavened bread made from all-purpose flour, and it's considered a treat rather than being eaten daily. In North America, you can buy both naan and chapattis from any Indian grocer and at many supermarkets. Most grocery stores also sell flatbreads, which can be heated and eaten just like chapattis. We equally enjoy a fresh baguette for soaking up curry sauces.

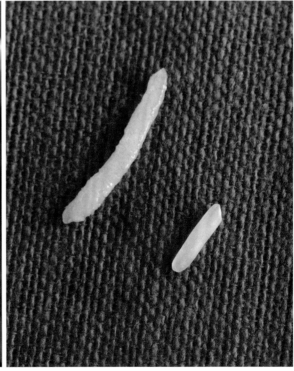

Naan

Cooked versus uncooked Basmati rice (see page 9)

CHICKPEA FLOUR is high in iron and fibre and has a slightly nutty taste. It is also gluten free. In India it's commonly used to make batter for pakoras (deep-fried vegetable fritters) and pura (savoury Indian crepes), and it is used as a flavoured thickener in curries and Indian desserts. Chickpea flour, which is made from black chickpeas, is known as *besan* and can be found at Indian grocers. It is not the same as garbanzo bean flour, which doesn't thicken as well and has a much milder flavour than besan. We do not recommend using garbanzo bean flour in our recipes.

COCONUT MILK is mostly used in Goa and southern India. We use the more expensive full-fat, premium coconut milk, which contains a very thick white cream at the top of the can and a flavourful water at the bottom. We stir these two parts together before adding the milk to our dishes. For us, low-fat coconut milk is too watery and lacks flavour, and coconut cream is too rich and makes a curry that risks becoming too sweet.

GHEE is clarified butter made by gently boiling butter and then straining out all the milk solids. The resulting liquid has a high heating temperature and can be used in place of any cooking oil in most recipes. In India, ghee has traditionally been expensive to buy and laborious to make (because families buy the milk, churn it to make butter and then boil the butter to make ghee). It is revered not only for its flavour (especially in lentil and vegetable curries) but also for its health properties (it is easily metabolized and digested), especially for growing children. Our recipe for ghee is on page 24.

LENTILS are known as *daal* in various Indian languages and are a staple food. They are an inexpensive source of iron, protein, B vitamins and fibre, which makes them a great substitute for meat, though we enjoy their flavour and texture enough that we'd eat them even without that excuse. In Indian homes, various lentil curries are a part of every dinner, no matter what else is served. There are many types of lentils, and most of them cook much faster than beans and have as many health benefits. They are easily digested, and they lower cholesterol and blood sugar. We much prefer soaking and cooking dried lentils, as canned or frozen ones are usually too mushy for our taste.

PANEER is a mild Indian cheese made from whole milk. It does not melt when it's heated, and you can add it to just about any vegetable dish or rice. Although you can buy readymade paneer from most Indian and South Asian grocers, it is easy to make at home once you get the hang of it. See our recipe on page 38.

RICE, BASMATI This is India's (and Pakistan's) rice. *Basmati* means that it is grown in the Himalayas, which gives the rice a special texture, aroma and length of grain. Indians are proud of our rice and we do not use Basmati rice produced anywhere else than in the Himalayas. When cooked properly, each grain will more than double in length; if you had the patience you could count each grain of cooked rice in your pot, as it is that flaky. Although Indian brown Basmati exists, the white Basmati is the most popular. While brown rice is healthier and full of B vitamins, iron and fibre, it also takes longer to digest. At home, we use both brown and white interchangeably. At our restaurants, we serve various brown and white Basmati pilafs.

SUGAR, RAW This sweetener, known as *gur*, is sugar cane juice boiled down to a coarse brown sugar. It is sold at Indian grocers as moist clumps or as a crumbly and moist sugar. Do not confuse palm sugar with raw sugar.

YOGURT is one of the most important foods in Indian cuisine. One reason most Indians are unable to accept a vegan diet is that we consider yogurt to be one of the healthiest foods. It's a source of calcium and all of the good bacteria that aid in digestion and keep our guts healthy. Indian food can be spicy, and yogurt is the perfect cooling complement. We also add yogurt to our masala sautés for a slightly tart flavour. Making your own yogurt, without any fancy gadgets, is one of the easiest things to do. Homemade yogurt won't have the firm texture of store-bought. See our recipe on page 34.

TIPS FOR INDIAN COOKING

If you are familiar with Indian cooking or you've cooked from one of our previous books, you will most likely know some or all of these secrets. If you are new to Indian recipes, these guidelines should help—but know that when you've made a recipe once, you can tweak it according to your own flavour and texture preferences.

1. A MASALA MEANS A MIXTURE OF SPICES—EITHER DRY OR WET.
A dry masala, such as Garam Masala (page 23), is a combination of ground spices that makes up one overall spicing profile. *Masala* can also refer to each spice you use in your curry (such as cumin, coriander, turmeric, cloves). A wet masala, on the other hand, is the basis of almost any Indian dish and is the equivalent of your stock for the curry.

Adding tumeric, ground cumin, salt, ground coriander and Ancho chili powder to a wet masala

It is a mixture of sautéed onions, garlic, tomatoes and spices. Once you get the hang of making a wet masala and recognizing when the oil is "glistening" on the tomatoes, you will find that making Indian food is simple. Most wet masalas are cooked on medium-high heat and come together in 10 to 12 minutes.

2. AROMATIC SPICES MAKE FLAVOURFUL CURRIES. Indian spices vary in intensity from brand to brand and they lose flavour the longer they sit on the shelf. Judge your spices by the strength of their aroma. If your cumin, coriander and Garam Masala (page 23) have only a very faint aroma, chances are you will not get a strong-flavoured curry. If you cook Indian food infrequently, we recommend that you buy whole seeds, store them in airtight containers and grind them fresh in a small coffee grinder before cooking. Seeds will keep for 6 months, if not longer. All spices should be kept in airtight containers in a dry, dark place at room temperature.

3. PREPARE YOUR INGREDIENTS BEFORE YOU START COOKING. All our recipes assume that you have washed and prepared the vegetables ahead of time. Peeling, coring, trimming, removing tough stems—do all this before you begin cooking.

4. DO NOT SKIMP ON THE OILS. In India, *khooshk* means "dry," and this doesn't just mean our skin and hair but also our insides. A dry inner body invites illness. Do not be put off by the amount of oil in our recipes. You need oil to cook your spices so they release their flavours and lose their raw taste. You need oil to sauté onions, garlic and ginger. You need oil to bind the various ingredients in your wet masala to create a rich, flavourful "sauce."

By "oils" we mean all-natural and healthy oils; we do not cook with hydrogenated or artificial oils. We prefer to cook with Ghee (page 24) or pure organic coconut oil at home, and we use olive, canola or grapeseed for non-Indian cooking. At the restaurants, we also use non-GMO canola or grapeseed oil. Since ghee and coconut oil solidify easily, we do not use them for marinated dishes. However, unlike vegetable and seed oils, they do not go rancid. They also have a very high heating temperature, or smoking point, so they are well suited for searing meats and fish, as well as for sautéing. Note that both ghee and coconut oil have a distinct flavour, so be sure that you like the taste of butter or a mild coconut flavour before using either oil. A family favourite is a fried egg or omelette cooked in either ghee or coconut oil.

5. SIZZLE YOUR SEEDS. Listen for this sound and look for the visual of the little seeds "boiling" in the heated oil. If your oil is not hot enough, it may take a minute or two for your seeds to begin to sizzle. We recommend that you allow them to sizzle for 15 seconds. The longer they sizzle, the more intense the flavour, as long as they don't burn.

6. ONIONS AND GARLIC ARE OPTIONAL (BUT HIGHLY RECOMMENDED). These vegetables are used copiously in Indian cooking, so we don't suggest you leave them both out of a dish, but you can decrease our suggested amounts according to your personal taste. You can use yellow, white or red onions, but we use red onions simply because in India a regular onion at the vegetable market is of the purple-red variety. We are also big fans of green onions, which we often add at the last minute as an additional layer to curries that aren't already onion heavy. We always use the entire green onion—the green parts are full of invaluable nutrients. We don't use shallots because they are delicate in flavour and don't match all of the spices. Shallots are expensive, and in our view it's better to cook with them in subtly flavoured dishes, most of which are not Indian. And don't fuss about the size of onions; if your "medium" or "large" is not the same as ours, that's okay. As long as it's within a general range, your results will be fine.

7. GIVE YOUR SAUTÉS SPACE. Onions need room in the pot to sauté properly. We use a pan 10 to 12 inches in diameter to make these recipes. Anything smaller is described in our recipes as a "small" frying pan or pot.

8. COOKING TIMES VARY. Every stove is different, and the diameter of the heat surface in relation to the pot can make your cooking times shorter or longer than the ones we've given here. If your cooking times are consistently longer—say, it always takes you a minute before your cumin seeds sizzle—do not worry. You may need to increase the heat slightly compared with what we've specified.

9. SALT AND CAYENNE ENHANCE THE FLAVOUR. These spices are very subjective. The amounts listed in the recipes are our personal preferences, but adjust the quantities according to your personal health rules and taste. We do feel that Indian food requires slightly more salt than other types of cooking to "bind" together the flavours of the various spices.

10. WHIPPING CREAM AND COCONUT MILK ARE OFTEN INTERCHANGE- ABLE. At home, we often skip the whipping cream or coconut milk in a recipe, unless they are crucial to the taste. (If a recipe is made with an onion/garlic/tomato masala, chances are you can skip the cream or coconut milk.) Whipping cream is usually used in northern Indian cuisine, and coconut milk is used in southern dishes. Not so in this cookbook. We include lots of recipes with coconut milk because not only does it create a thicker, velvety texture and flavour, it is also vegan and ideal for those who are lactose intolerant. It's also a nice change from the typical cream. Nevertheless, we are lovers of cream!

11. PRESSURE COOKERS SAVE TIME AND ENERGY. For those who love legumes and brown and wild rices, a pressure cooker can save a lot of time and money, as organic bulk items are cheaper than precooked frozen or canned foods. A pressure cooker is a sealed, airtight pot that cooks foods quickly with steam. It is great for curries because you can sauté your masala in the pressure cooker, which allows you to cook everything in a single pot. And because it saves cooking time, a pressure cooker also saves energy.

Once you try a pressure cooker, you'll never go back to buying canned legumes or soaking dried ones overnight. (Or you can continue to soak your legumes and then pressure-cook them for one-quarter of the suggested cooking time.) The cooking times in our recipes are based on our own Indian pressure cooker, which we use regularly. Since different models use different amounts of pressure, follow the times suggested in the instructions for your own model.

12. GIVE CILANTRO A TRY. This fresh herb is used copiously in Indian cuisine. We always use both the leaves and the tender stems in our recipes, unless otherwise stated. Cut off and discard only the tougher part of the stems at the very bottom, but otherwise the stems add flavour and texture. If you truly dislike cilantro, you can always leave it out of the recipe.

MEASUREMENTS

When trying a recipe for the first time, measuring accurately is important. It can give you confidence that the dish will turn out properly, and it provides an idea of the flavours and textures you're looking for. Indian cooking does not have to be precise—unless you want it to be.

Meeru and her kitchen staff measure ingredients using whatever spoons are handy. At home and at cooking events, if Vikram is making small amounts, he often adds spices with his fingers. Both our daughters cook, but whereas Nanaki cooks out of necessity and likes to be precise because she wants her cooking to taste "like it's supposed to," Shanik enjoys cooking leisurely and doesn't have the patience to level out measurements. She guesses at the amounts, and even if the result isn't perfect, she's convinced that it's *actually pretty good*. All four of us can make the same dish using the same spices but using different amounts of them, and all four versions will taste good.

The bottom line is that precise amounts of spices don't matter, once you get the hang of a recipe and know what you like and don't like. It's okay to vary the quantity by 10 to 15 per cent in either direction, though we generally suggest that you don't use less than the recommended amount until you have made the dish at least once. Most important, note that adding more onions or vegetables means the spice level will go down.

We are always comparing various Indian recipes and are often amused by the variation in spice measurements. One cook's chicken curry will call for 1 teaspoon of a particular spice while another's will call for 1 tablespoon. When more instinctive Indian cooks tell us their recipes, we are often told to "use some cumin and coriander." When we ask how much, the response is often: "When it looks and smells right." Even getting specific measurements from our own mothers is practically impossible. If we push Vikram's mother for measurements, she will just look at us as if to say: use what you like, for goodness sake! While cooking with instinct has a certain romanticism about it, we understand that it's difficult when learning a new cuisine.

One day in 2014, Oguz Istif, the chief financial officer of our Vij's companies, brought his twenty-four-year-old niece to our home. She was visiting Vancouver from Turkey to learn English, and she cooked us a big Turkish meal. Meeru hoped to learn some Turkish recipes and was working as her helper. A fast and instinctive cook, Oguz's niece was making a Turkish-style chocolate cake for dessert. When it was time to add the flour, she poured it directly from the bag into the mixing bowl with the wet ingredients. She would stir, and add more flour. When Meeru asked why she wasn't measuring the flour, she looked confused and said that she *was* measuring: "When the batter feels the same softness of my earlobe, I'll know it's the right amount of flour." (Shanik was amused and whispered that she hoped it was a soft and cushiony earlobe.) Although Meeru didn't learn how to cook anything Turkish that evening, we had a delicious meal, including the cake.

Our recipes here give you a starting point, but remember, Indian cooking does not have to be precise!

WINE PAIRINGS WITH INDIAN FOOD

Both Meeru and (especially) Vikram love to drink wine. And while many people believe that beer is the best drink to have with spicy foods like curry, we believe that the right wine pairing can provide an equally enjoyable experience.

Vikram is a certified sommelier, but for the past ten years, our wine director and chief operating officer, Mike Bernardo, has overseen the wine program at our restaurants. He is knowledgeable and incredibly passionate about pairing wines with our complex and layered foods. In general, he finds that youthful, fresh and crisp white wines with not too much oak work well with Indian food. And as for reds, medium-bodied, low-tannin selections are ideal. Having said that, everyone has their own preferences, so the key to making a great selection is knowing which wine profiles you enjoy personally. Keep in mind that cheap wines are not always bad and expensive wines are not always great.

We asked Mike to provide some examples of the kinds of wines that pair well with our dishes, based on the preferences of some of our various Vij's staff. Their knowledge of wine ranges from limited to extensive. Although Mike has noted the specific wines they enjoy (to illustrate the particular profiles of those wines), there are plenty of other winemakers who produce the same style of wine. Don't limit yourself to buying the wines listed below, but use them as guidelines. Specific years are not given because the point here is to talk more about flavour profiles.

MEERU In general, Meeru prefers crisp whites with mineral flavours and smooth reds, no matter what she's eating. She's more concerned with "not drinking bad alcohol if it's going in my body." She has one sentence for reds she doesn't enjoy: "This tastes like vinegary grape juice and hurts my chest." If she doesn't like a white wine, her comment is, "This is oily."

Preferred red: For her usual drinking, Meeru enjoys Bodegas Filon Garnacha from Spain. This is an inexpensive wine made from Grenache grapes, with cassis and cherry on the palate and with a cleansing pop of acid on the finish that doesn't compete with spices. Her special red is the Vietti Perbacco from the Langhe region in northern Italy. This is an absolute gem of an earthy, rustic wine made from Nebbiolo grapes. I recommend that you decant this wine to let it open for an hour. It's a powerful wine at first but softens to velvety smoothness. Meeru usually stops drinking any wine by the time she is midway through her meal, as she finds the combination of alcohol and Indian spices too heavy after a certain point. Not so with the Vietti Perbacco.

Preferred white: While she may not know the details of their *terroir* or specific grape varietals, Meeru loves Godello wines from Valdeorras in eastern Galicia (northwestern Spain). The Godello grape is sometimes compared with the Chardonnay grape of Burgundy, France. While Chardonnay is the most popular white wine in North America, Godello is relatively

Oguz and Vikram

unknown. Like Chardonnay, the taste of Godello depends much on whether it was aged in oak or steel. Meeru has been consistent in her dislike of oaky, buttery Chardonnays ("too oily with Indian spices"), and her love of Godello from Valdeorras reinforces her preference, as these wines are often aged in steel and have a crisp, lively and mineral taste.

VIKRAM Vikram gravitates to all full-bodied wines, red or white, with Indian food.

Preferred red: Vikram insists he doesn't have a favourite red and just prefers "any full-bodied Cabernet Sauvignon." Having spent many nights drinking with Vikram after work, I can say that one wine he particularly enjoys is Ehlers Estate 1886 Cabernet Sauvignon from St. Helena in Napa Valley, California. He likes the rich, bold, black fruit-forward flavours of New World Cabernets, and he thoroughly enjoys this California Cabernet with Mildly Curried Beef Short Ribs (page 211) served with Roasted Spicy Okra with Walnuts and Jelly Beans (page 94).

Preferred white: Vikram comes in with a fantastic pick: Schloss Gobelsburg Grüner Veltliner from Austria. Like the Godellos, Grüner Veltliner wines can range from full bodied (like Chardonnay, minus the butter and oak finish) to mineral crisp (like Sauvignon Blanc). Vikram's choice is full bodied with slight mineral notes on the mid palate and a complexly layered and brightly acidic finish. This is my favourite white wine to go with our lamb popsicles, however they are spiced. The Lamb Popsicles with Garlic and Ricotta-Fenugreek Topping (page 218) can be tricky to pair with certain wines, but Schloss Gobelsburg Grüner Veltliner is the perfect match.

OGUZ ISTIF, CHIEF FINANCIAL OFFICER Oguz is Turkish, and although his cuisine has many similarities to Indian food, it isn't as spicy hot. Several varieties of sun-dried chili peppers (Kirmizi, Maras and Urfa are popular) are a mainstay of the Turkish palate. Turkish peppers provide an earthy and not so searing heat. Oguz's taste in wine reflects his love of both Turkish and Indian cuisine.

Preferred red: Oguz's pick is Torre d'Orti Valpolicella, an Italian wine made by drying Corvina, Rondinella and Molinara grapes in small wooden trays. This results in a well-balanced complex and spicy wine. Many Valpolicellas are too big and rich for Indian food, but this particular wine has more of a fruit-forward freshness of mixed berries with a hint of white pepper.

Preferred white: Oguz chooses the Weingut Knoll Grüner Veltliner, which is at the opposite end of the spectrum from Vikram's choice. Oguz prefers the intense stone and mineral finish that can be described as a combination of Sauvignon Blanc and dry Riesling.

DEANNA ANDERSON, MANAGER, VIJ'S, AND CORY MCPHEE, MANAGER, RANGOLI Like Meeru, Deanna likes lighter, crisper wines. In contrast, Cory enjoys bold flavours in food and wine.

Preferred reds: Deanna's favourite is Sokol Blosser Pinot Noir from Oregon. This is a light and refreshing red wine that has a lovely hint of fruit without any juicy sweetness. For those like Deanna and Meeru who don't like a cacophony of what they deem competing flavours of spice and wine, this Pinot Noir is like a thin silk rug that carries the spices.

Cory goes the opposite route with Ravenswood Zinfandel from California. Zinfandels are spicy wines and many of them are very high in alcohol content, which can cause an unpleasant heat reaction on your palate when combined with spicy food. For this reason, I am very careful in selecting Zinfandels. Cory's choice is from our Rangoli menu, and it has a good balance between spicy and fruity, with an acidic finish. Both Oguz's Torre d'Orti Valpolicella selection and Cory's Zinfandel are big concentrated wines with a similar flavour profile, but the Valpolicella is lighter. Cory's red selection makes sense, given his love of bolder flavours.

Preferred whites: Both Deanna and Cory choose sparkling white wines as their first choice, but the similarities end there. Deanna prefers any of the light, crisp and dry Italian Proseccos, whereas Cory specifically goes for the richer Paul Zinck Crémant d'Alsace, which has a strong apricot fruit on the nose and palate.

MIKE BERNARDO I want to mention here that many staff also included Rieslings and British Columbia white wines in their lists. I didn't include them above because they are also among my personal favourites (see below).

Preferred red: I land in the Rhône Valley of France, with Perrin & Fils Château de Beaucastel from Châteauneuf-du-Pape as one of my favourites. Although there is an array of wines coming from the Rhône Valley, I prefer the *terroir* (the soil, geography and climate of a land) and grapes—mostly Grenache, Syrah and Mourvèdre—of the Châteauneuf-du-Pape sub-region in the southern Rhône Valley. Older vintages of this wine will have softer tannins and smoothness. These are also full-bodied wines with hints of dark fruit (currants and blueberries) and dark spices (cloves).

If you are unfamiliar with Rhône Valley wines, Perrin & Fils Côtes du Rhône Villages from the northern Rhône Valley is an easy-drinking, lighter wine that is the perfect starting point and goes universally with most of the recipes in this book. We generally serve this particular wine by the glass at all of our restaurants.

Preferred whites: I have an expensive obsession with Krug Champagne. I love its rich, full body, its toasted bread flavour and its constantly rejuvenating tiny, unobtrusive bubbles that cleanse your palate throughout the meal. It's a great complement for all the layers of spices in our cuisine.

Another standout white, which Meeru also enjoys, is Poplar Grove Pinot Gris from Naramata Bench in British Columbia. This white is fully rounded, with fresh tropical fruit flavours, without being overly sweet. I agree with Meeru when she says it is "gently sweet, with elegant heft."

I also have a soft spot for Riesling with Indian food. There are many styles of Riesling, with the German ones having more residual sugar with high acidity and the British Columbia ones being bone-dry with cleansing citrus notes. If you ever get the chance to compare the two styles, it's a wonderful example of how *terroir* influences the taste of wine grapes.

Although one of my favourite Rieslings is the German J. J. Prüm Graacher Himmelreich Kabinett, much to my and Vikram's chagrin Meeru finds all German Rieslings too sweet and "oily." She does, however, like B.C. Rieslings, including my favourite, from Tantalus Vineyards. In 2015 I created a signature wine, called Mike B.'s Riesling Cabinett, at the Okanagan Crush Pad winery in British Columbia. I crafted it to go specifically with Indian cuisine. I made this Riesling in stainless steel and concrete tanks for a mineral style with a crisp lemon-and-lime finish, and we offer it by the bottle at Vij's. It complements both light vegetarian dishes and spicy red meat curries.

The more you know and drink wine, the more you will come to know your own preferences. Vikram, for example, drinks what he personally enjoys, and the wines he drinks are not necessarily the ones a wine magazine would suggest as a match with spicy Indian food. If you're less confident about your choices, stick with white wines that have crisp, mineral, citrus notes, or with reds that are smooth, soft on tannins and lightly sweet.

Mike B.'s Riesling Cabinett

CONDIMENTS

AND

COMPLEMENTS

EAT YOUR SALAD!

At home and at our restaurants, we rarely serve an Indian meal without some sort of accompaniment, such as chutney or raita or sprouted lentils or raw chopped vegetables. We don't really have a name for these dishes, as they are just an automatic addition to our meals, but in this book we call them condiments and complements.

In both the Vij and Dhalwala homes when we were growing up, no dinner was served without a crunchy "salad" of cut-up cucumber, daikon, carrots and tomatoes sprinkled with a bit of salt, pepper and lemon. (In the Dhalwala home in the U.S., we added celery.) As much as Indian cooking involves oil, adding oil of any kind to this salad was considered food blasphemy. In addition to salad, Vikram's parents would allow him to sprinkle *ghatia* (deep-fried and spiced chickpea flour, a bit like potato chips) on his curries once or twice a week. There were always various chutneys in the fridge, and Vikram's mom loved these and pickled ginger with her meal. At a minimum, Meeru's mom always served some form of pickle alongside the salad.

When Vikram first left home to go to Austria for hotel management school, he packed a big jar of mango pickle and bags of ghatia in his suitcase. Once those pickles and ghatia ran out, he was resigned to not having any Indian flavours with his Austrian meals at school. It's a loss he has never quite forgotten, and to this day he enjoys (even insists on!) his ghatia and pickle with Indian meals. (If you want to try ghatia for yourself, you can visit an Indian grocer and choose from among various flavours, but we recommend you try the healthy and delicious spiced pumpkin seeds instead.)

Except for the Garam Masala, Ghee and Tamarind Paste, which are wonderful complements in your Indian cooking, the recipes in this section are meant to be served at the table with anything you prepare in this book. Garam masala is not really a necessity like, say, cumin, but if you make it, you can sprinkle it on any curry or your plain yogurt or even on your raw vegetable salad with a bit of lemon. Ghee and tamarind paste can also be added in place of, or in addition to, other ingredients. And don't forget about the "salad"—simply cut up whatever salad vegetables you enjoy and sprinkle in some lemon, salt and pepper (be generous with all three). This may not sound very appetizing, but try it with your curries and you may just find this to be the most refreshing complement of all.

GARAM MASALA

We have been cooking with our signature garam masala, which means "warm spice mixture," for more than twenty years. The special ingredient is the seed from the black cardamom pod. From the outside, you can't always tell whether the seeds inside are good, so always buy more pods than your recipe calls for. Gently crush the pods with the side of a knife, peel back the shell with your fingers and release the seeds. The ideal pod will contain dark brown to almost black, moist seeds that are stuck together. Discard any lighter brown or very dry seeds.

Fresh spices make a big difference to the aroma and flavour of Indian cooking. Try to buy all the whole spices for this recipe at the same time. Whole roasted spices will last for about 6 months in an airtight container, but don't worry if yours have been around a bit longer. Meeru recently found a year-old tin of garam masala in the house, and it was still fresher than most store-bought garam masalas. She used it and no one noticed.

In our previous cookbooks we included nutmeg and mace in the recipe, but we've decided that as long as you have strong spices, a garam masala without these two ingredients is also great. Plus, for home cooks who are relatively new to Indian cooking, just a tiny bit too much of either one of those can ruin your spice mixture.

6 tablespoons cumin seeds

1 tablespoon pounded cinnamon sticks

½ tablespoon whole cloves

½ tablespoon black cardamom seeds (from 10 to 14 whole pods)

MAKES ½ CUP

PREP & COOKING TIME: 10 MINUTES + 20 MINUTES TO COOL

TURN ON YOUR stovetop exhaust fan. In a small, heavy-bottomed frying pan, heat the cumin seeds, cinnamon pieces, cloves and cardamom seeds on medium to high heat, stirring constantly. When the cumin seeds darken, in 5 to 8 minutes, immediately transfer the roasted spices to a bowl. Allow them to cool for 20 minutes.

Place the roasted spices in a spice (or coffee) grinder and grind until the mixture has the consistency of store-bought black pepper. Will keep in an airtight container in a dark place for up to 6 months.

GHEE (CLARIFIED BUTTER)

1 pound organic unsalted butter

Ghee is butter that has been gently boiled until it separates, and then all the milk solids are removed in a sieve or with a fine-slotted spoon and discarded. The clear, golden liquid that's left is highly valued—in small to moderate amounts—for its rich, nutty flavour and its nutritional content. Unlike chemically produced vegetable oils or animal fats, ghee is easily metabolized and digested. Most important for Indians, it is vegetarian.

We use ghee as a cooking oil in vegetarian curries, but it can be used instead of cooking oil in virtually any recipe because of its very high smoking point. We don't use ghee, however, when cooking red meat curries or dishes made with whipping cream because the fat in those foods is already rich enough. But ghee tastes great in a simple chicken curry, and our Mild Turmeric and Ghee Chicken Curry (page 192) is a lovely, mild yet flavourful comfort food that children—or those who prefer less-spicy food—particularly enjoy. You can also drizzle warmed ghee on top of rice pilafs, breads, and lentil or vegetable curries.

Ghee and turmeric are especially valued in Ayurvedic cooking for their medicinal properties. We introduced organic homemade ghee and turmeric to Nanaki and Shanik's diets when they were nine months old. Their "baby food" was ½ cup white rice, ½ cup mung beans, 1 tablespoon ghee, ½ teaspoon turmeric and ½ teaspoon salt. Since it was baby food we just cooked it, covered, until it was a mushy texture. When Nanaki was born, she was covered with eczema and a lot of body hair. To nourish her granddaughter's skin, Meeru's mother gave Nanaki daily massages with a combination of ghee and turmeric, while Meeru complained about the smell in their small apartment and worried that her mother would break one of Nanaki's tiny bones.

In fact, ghee has a long history in Meeru's family. Before the Partition of India in 1947, which divided greater India into the countries of India and Pakistan, both of Meeru's parents' families lived in what is now Pakistan. There they ate ghee every day because the raw milk from which it was made was readily available. However, both families were displaced by violence in August 1947, and while her mother's family was able to re-establish themselves in India, her father's family were refugees and lived in the refugee camp in Old Delhi. There the Indian government gave food rations of flour, lentils, powdered eggs (sent from the U.S. government) and a small tin of Dalda, which is an artificial hydrogenated oil, much like shortening but used like ghee. For the five years that Meeru's father lived in the refugee camp with his grandparents, he did not eat ghee. When she could finally afford to buy raw milk, his grandmother started to make ghee again—churning the milk by hand into butter and then boiling it to separate the solids from the fat. She would make Meeru's father drink a cup of lightly warmed raw milk with a tablespoon of ghee and some sugar, with a side of a fresh boiled egg, until "he became a strong man." The beauty of this story is that most refugee families displaced during the partition have a similar version of this story to tell.

To this day, Hindus who can afford it give the gift of a jar of ghee to the temple priest, who uses it as incense by adding it to the temple "fireplace." For prayers at home, Hindus place ghee and a wick in a small earthen clay pot (called a *diya*) and use it as a candle, as ghee is known to purify the air.

MAKES 2 CUPS

PREP & COOKING TIME: 20 MINUTES

MELT THE BUTTER in a small, heavy-bottomed pot on medium heat. Allow it to boil gently, and as the milk solids foam up on top, remove and discard them with a small, fine-mesh sieve. Keep skimming the foam from the top for about 15 minutes, or until only golden liquid remains. This is ghee. Allow the ghee to cool for 15 to 20 minutes.

While the ghee is cooling, wash and dry a 1-pint mason jar with a tight-fitting lid. Pour the cool liquid into the jar and tightly close the lid. Will keep at room temperature for up to a month or, better yet, refrigerated for up to 6 months.

TAMARIND PASTE

3 ½ to 4 ½ cups water

1 package (14 ounces) pure seedless tamarind (*imli*)

While you can buy tamarind paste at Indian grocers and some supermarkets, many prepared versions contain sugar and spices. This recipe requires less effort than the ones in our previous books because it's not as concentrated, which is perfect for the recipes in this book. You will need anywhere from 3 ½ cups to 4 ½ cups water—basically more water will mean less concentrated. But you do need enough liquid to strain the boiled tamarind through the sieve. Add 1 or 2 tablespoons of this paste to Date Chutney (page 28) for an added tartness; it is also used for making the pani (tamarind water) in the Pani-puri (page 56).

MAKES 2 CUPS

PREP & COOKING TIME: 40 MINUTES

COMBINE THE WATER and tamarind in a medium pot and bring to a boil on medium-high heat. Reduce the heat to medium, cover and boil for 20 minutes, stirring the tamarind every 5 minutes to break it into small pieces. Remove the pot from the heat and allow the mixture to cool, uncovered, for 30 minutes.

Place a fine-mesh sieve over a bowl. Strain the tamarind mixture, using the back of a metal spoon to push the flesh through the sieve and into the bowl. The less you scrape the tamarind, the runnier the paste will be and the milder its flavour. For a concentrated paste, keep scraping the tamarind with the spoon (or use your hands) until only the skins and a few seeds are left in the sieve. Discard these solids. The resulting paste should have the consistency of thick applesauce. Will keep refrigerated in an airtight container for up to 10 days or frozen indefinitely.

SOUR CREAM DRESSING

This dressing is an easy mainstay in our daily cooking at Vij's and Rangoli, where we use it as a condiment or chutney. At Rangoli, we make it for a pulled pork curry, and at Vij's, we serve it with the Beet Bites (page 51), using green onions since there's already garlic in that dish. (Regular onions are too strong for this recipe.) This dressing is also great in hamburgers and in place of mayonnaise for dipping french fries. Depending on your love of garlic, use between ½ and 1 teaspoon.

MAKES 1 CUP

PREP TIME: 10 MINUTES + 15 MINUTES TO CHILL

IN A MEDIUM BOWL, mix together all the ingredients. Cover and refrigerate for at least 15 minutes. Will keep refrigerated in an airtight container for up to 1 week.

1 cup full-fat sour cream

1 teaspoon ground cumin OR dried green fenugreek leaves

½ teaspoon ground cayenne pepper

½ to 1 teaspoon finely chopped garlic OR 1 tablespoon finely chopped green onions, white part only

½ teaspoon salt

DATE CHUTNEY

2 pounds fresh Medjool dates (no need to pit them)

½ pound dried Mission or other dark figs

6 cups water

10 whole cloves

2 tablespoons chopped ginger

1 tablespoon salt

1 teaspoon ground cayenne pepper

We have been making date chutney for years and serving it with our meat and (especially) deep-fried vegetarian foods at Vij's and Rangoli. This similar-tasting version contains fewer ingredients but it does take time to make, so we recommend that you cook up a large batch and freeze whatever you don't eat right away. You can also halve this recipe, but use 4 cups water instead of 3.

Date chutney tastes great on everything. Try it as a spread on cheddar cheese, in our Fruit Chaat (page 72) and under Lamb Loin with Sautéed Bell Peppers and Sunchokes (page 216).

MAKES 3 ½ TO 4 CUPS

PREP & COOKING TIME: 1 ½ HOURS

COMBINE ALL the ingredients in a large pot and bring to a boil on high heat. Reduce the heat to medium-low and simmer, uncovered, for 40 minutes, stirring regularly. Remove the pot from the heat and allow the chutney to cool for 30 minutes.

Place a fine-mesh sieve over a large bowl. Strain the spicy fruit mixture through the sieve and into the bowl. Using your hands, knead and press the fruit into the bowl until only the dried skins, pits and ginger are left in the sieve. Compost or discard these solids. The resulting date chutney should have the rough consistency of ketchup. Season with more salt, if needed. Will keep refrigerated in an airtight container for up to 10 days or frozen indefinitely.

LEMON PICKLE

Of all the pickles we serve in the restaurants, this one is the easiest to make at home. It's also our favourite, since it's pretty and adds a light tartness to heavier spices. We leave the skins on the lemons because they have nutritional value, so we use thin-skinned organic lemons. The thinner the skin, the better for this pickle. In India, all lemons are tiny and green, like our limes in North America, but we prefer the flavour of the yellow lemon in this recipe.

Pickling involves allowing the ingredients to ferment for a few days to preserve them and develop their flavour. Indian pickles are meant to be made in the sun, which softens the ingredients. If you have a sunny kitchen counter, it will take three full days to make this pickle. If you don't, then give it four days and accept that your lemon pickle will not be as soft. It will soften up as it stays in the fridge.

Bacteria grow very quickly on preservative-free pickles (you will smell it, so don't worry about not noticing!), so always use a clean utensil rather than potentially dirty fingers to take a pickle from the jar. Our mothers kept various pickles in the cupboard for months and would slap our hands really hard if they caught us using our fingers. Serve this pickle as a condiment with everything and anything, as we do at our restaurants.

MAKES 1 QUART

PREP TIME: 20 MINUTES + 3 TO 4 DAYS TO SET

6 organic thin-skinned lemons, unpeeled, each cut into 8 wedges and seeded

¼ cup grapeseed oil

1 teaspoon kalonji seeds

1 tablespoon salt

1 tablespoon sugar

1 teaspoon crushed cayenne pepper OR 4 whole dried cayenne peppers, cut in half lengthwise

continued...

WASH A 1-QUART mason jar with a tight-fitting lid in very hot water and dry it well. Lightly squeeze a small amount of lemon juice from each of the lemon wedges into the jar. Place all the pieces of lemon into the jar as well.

Heat the grapeseed oil in a small frying pan on medium-high heat for 1 minute. Sprinkle in the kalonji seeds and allow them to sizzle for 30 seconds. Immediately pour all the oil and seeds into the mason jar with the lemons. Add the salt, sugar and cayenne. Close the jar tightly and shake it well, until everything is really well mixed together. Take off the lid and allow the jar to sit, uncovered, for 5 minutes so the oil can cool. Replace the lid, sealing the jar tightly, and place it on a windowsill, preferably in the sun, for 24 hours.

Shake the jar well again. Repeat this daily shake for 2 more days if your jar is in the sun or for 3 more days if it is not. Refrigerate the pickles until cool.

Open the jar and, using a fork, pull out one of the pickles. Taste a small piece. If it's way too tart, add more salt to the jar, ½ teaspoon at a time, shake, and taste another small piece. Reseal the jar and refrigerate until needed. Will keep refrigerated in a sealed mason jar for up to 1 month (the longer they are in the fridge, the softer they become).

SPICED PICKLE-LIKE CARROTS

¼ cup coconut oil

½ tablespoon kalonji seeds

1 bunch green onions, white and green parts separated and finely chopped

¼ cup puréed fresh or canned tomatoes

1 tablespoon ground cumin

2 teaspoons mango powder (break up any clumps)

½ tablespoon ground coriander OR ½ teaspoon ground fenugreek seeds

1 teaspoon turmeric

1 teaspoon ground cayenne pepper

1 teaspoon salt (to taste)

11 ounces carrots, sliced 3 inches long and ½ inch wide

2 teaspoons brown sugar

In India, carrots are marinated in lots of mustard oil with vinegar, salt and kalonji seeds to make a pickle. While we love authentic pickled carrots, they are not very popular with our customers. This version, though still very Indian, is inexplicably far more popular with North Americans and much faster to prepare. Feel free to add bite-sized pieces of cauliflower florets to this recipe, or replace the carrots with cauliflower.

We don't want too many spices to hide the crunch and taste of the vegetables, so we recommend that you use either the coriander or the fenugreek rather than both. The coriander is more floral, whereas the fenugreek is a bit more tart with a curry flavour. At the restaurants, we serve these carrots warm, in small bowls, as a condiment. If you're reheating them, 1 minute in a microwave oven on medium power works well.

SERVES 6 TO 8 AS A CONDIMENT

PREP & COOKING TIME: 30 MINUTES

HEAT THE OIL in a medium, heavy-bottomed pan on high heat for 1 minute. Sprinkle in the kalonji seeds, stir and allow the seeds to sizzle for 45 seconds. Add the whites of the green onions, stir well and sauté for 2 minutes. Add the tomatoes, cumin, mango powder, coriander (or fenugreek), turmeric, cayenne and salt; stir again. Sauté for 2 minutes. Reduce the heat to medium and add the carrots, mixing them into the spices. Cook for 5 minutes, or until the carrots are cooked but still crunchy. Stir in the sugar and cook for another 30 seconds. Remove from the heat and stir in the green part of the green onions. Transfer to a small bowl. Serve with a small fork so everyone can serve themselves at the table. Will keep refrigerated in a mason jar for up to 1 week. Reheat before serving, as the coconut oil will solidify in the fridge.

RAITA, THREE WAYS

Raita is a staple with just about every meal. The basic version is just yogurt, cucumber and salt, but at home we make several variations just for the fun of it. Shanik doesn't eat yogurt, period, but Vikram, Meeru and Nanaki eat it every day, almost like a cold soup. In the summer, try serving raita as you would a gazpacho.

MAKES 2 CUPS

PREP TIME: 15 MINUTES + 1 HOUR TO CHILL (OPTIONAL)

CUCUMBER RAITA In a small bowl, combine the yogurt, cucumber and salt until well mixed. Add your choice of optional ingredients. Serve immediately or refrigerate, covered, until chilled, about 1 hour. Will keep refrigerated in an airtight container for up to 1 week. (It will not keep as long as plain yogurt because of the added fresh ingredients.)

CARROT–BELL PEPPER RAITA Follow the method for the cucumber raita (including your choice of optional ingredients), replacing the cucumber with the carrots and bell peppers.

NANAKI'S FAVOURITE "RAITA" In a small bowl, combine the yogurt, pears and salt until well mixed. Stir in the cilantro and coriander. Serve immediately. Will keep refrigerated in an airtight container for up to 4 days, depending on the texture of the pears.

CUCUMBER RAITA

2 cups plain yogurt (page 34)

1 medium to large cucumber, unpeeled, grated

1 teaspoon salt

1 tomato, chopped (optional)

½ cup chopped cilantro (optional)

1 teaspoon toasted cumin seeds OR ground cumin (optional)

½ teaspoon ground cayenne pepper (optional)

CARROT–BELL PEPPER RAITA

2 carrots, lightly peeled and grated

1 to 2 green or red bell peppers, finely chopped

NANAKI'S FAVOURITE "RAITA"

2 cups plain yogurt (page 34)

2 Bartlett pears, unpeeled, grated

1 teaspoon salt

¼ cup finely chopped cilantro

1 teaspoon ground coriander

PLAIN YOGURT

4 cups whole milk (organic is best)

1 tablespoon of your favourite natural and preservative-free plain yogurt

Making your own yogurt is a great way to save money—especially if you usually buy organic—but we're also convinced that homemade has more probiotics than store-bought yogurt. Probiotics are the helpful bacteria that keep our guts healthy, and this is one of the main reasons we eat so much yogurt in India, except we call it "digestion." Eating yogurt with spicy and spiced foods is how children learn to tolerate them, as the yogurt gently cools the palate. The next best food for cooling the palate when eating Indian food is cucumber. This is why raita—yogurt and cucumber at its most basic—is often served with spicy dishes (see page 33).

At some organic grocers, you can buy organic un-homogenized whole milk, which we highly recommend for making yogurt. The flavour of the yogurt comes from the flavour of the milk itself. When Meeru's parents moved from India to the United States, they missed the flavour of the yogurt they were used to. They considered everything on offer at the grocery stores in Virginia to be *bukwaz* (crap). So on a trip to visit relatives in India, Meeru's mother visited Mahesh uncle (see page 82) in New Delhi and brought back half a cup of the yogurt made in his house. She used that yogurt as a starter, and the yogurt she made in the States tasted very close to the yogurt from New Delhi. She's now been making yogurt from that same starter for more than fifteen years. (Once you've made yogurt, you can save a tablespoon to begin your next batch.)

Nanaki has always loved plain yogurt on just about everything. When Meeru and Vikram took her to Montreal for her first year at McGill University, the first thing Vikram did was to find a co-op that sold organic, local, grass-fed yogurt made from un-homogenized milk and he made sure that her weekly food budget included this expensive purchase. He figured that as long as she ate a bowl of yogurt, it didn't matter how much alcohol she drank. While she isn't going to reveal to her parents how much she partied, she has plenty reassured us that she did, in fact, eat a large bowl of yogurt every day. We have since taught her how to make her own.

At home, we make our yogurt in a stainless steel pot with a lid. We don't take the temperature of our milk when heating and cooling it: we simply bring the milk to a boil, then immediately remove it from the heat, before it starts to rise and boil over. Remember that homemade yogurt won't have the firm, jelly-like texture of store-bought, so you usually need to stir it smooth before serving.

MAKES 3 TO 4 CUPS

PREP TIME: A VERY EASY 45 MINUTES TO 1 HOUR TO MAKE + 10 TO 12 HOURS TO SET

POUR THE MILK into a medium-large, heavy-bottomed pot. Without stirring, bring it just to the boiling point on medium-high heat, then immediately remove the pot from the heat. Allow the milk to cool for 30 minutes. Once the milk is lukewarm to the touch (we describe it as "the temperature of a baby's bathwater"), gently stir in the yogurt and cover the pot.

If your oven does not emit heat when it is turned off, place the rack at its lowest level in the oven, set the pot on the rack and close the door. Leave the oven off. Alternatively, wrap the pot in a small blanket and allow it to sit on the counter. You want the same temperature you use when allowing bread dough to rise. Allow the mixture to set for 10 to 12 hours. (If you still have liquid milk after this time, scrap this batch and start again. The temperature was likely too warm and your yogurt has not, and will not, set.)

Will keep refrigerated in an airtight container for up to 2 weeks. (Yogurt will not go bad after 2 weeks, but its flavour will become more sour.)

BENGALI-STYLE CURRY
(VEGAN AND VEGETARIAN OPTIONS)

VEGAN CURRY

⅓ cup cooking oil

1 tablespoon all-purpose flour

1 ½ tablespoons ground panch poran

3 cups puréed fresh or canned tomatoes (6 to 7 medium)

1 teaspoon turmeric

1 teaspoon crushed cayenne pepper

1 teaspoon salt

5 cups water

CREAMY VEGETARIAN CURRY

¼ cup cooking oil

2 tablespoons ground panch poran

3 cups puréed fresh or canned tomatoes (6 to 7 medium)

1 teaspoon turmeric

1 teaspoon crushed cayenne pepper

1 teaspoon salt

4 cups water

1 cup whipping cream

This distinct-tasting curry is one of our most popular spice mixtures, and it is often on the menu at Vij's and Rangoli. Unlike garam masala, which can taste different with each batch, panch poran—the Bengali spice mixture used in this curry—tastes the same each time. We purchase the premixed whole-seed masala from our Indian grocer and grind it at home or at the restaurants. There is no need to pre-roast, as the panch poran will be cooked in hot oil.

We have been making this curry with whipping cream for years, and we serve it with a variety of dishes, such as our Simple Grilled Chicken (page 190). At home, Meeru often likes a bowl of rice with lots of Bengali curry and Sprouted Lentils (page 42) sprinkled on top. Vikram loves to cook bone-in beef short ribs in this creamy sauce for about 1 ½ hours. The vegan version of this curry makes a rich vegetarian meal served with the Savoury Indian Truffles (page 62) and Zucchini, Squash and Potato Sauté (page 106).

SERVES 6 (MAKES 6 TO 8 CUPS)
PREP & COOKING TIME: 20 MINUTES (VEGAN);
15 MINUTES (VEGETARIAN)

VEGAN CURRY Heat the oil in a medium pot on medium-high heat and stir in the flour. Cook for 3 to 4 minutes, stirring constantly like you're making a roux, until the flour is a slightly darker gold colour. Add the panch poran and cook, stirring, for 2 to 3 minutes, or until the spices begin to sizzle and foam. They will be a darker gold colour. Immediately add the tomatoes and stir to prevent the panch poran from burning. Stir in the turmeric, cayenne and salt. Sauté the masala for 5 minutes, or until the oil glistens on the tomatoes. Stir in the water and cook the mixture until the curry comes to a boil. Reduce the heat to low and simmer for 5 minutes, or until little droplets of oil glisten on top and the curry has thickened slightly. Serve hot. Will keep refrigerated in an airtight container for up to 1 week.

CREAMY CURRY Heat the oil in a medium pot on medium-high heat for 1 minute. Sprinkle in the panch poran and allow it to sizzle for 10 to 15 seconds. It will foam up. Immediately add the tomatoes and stir to prevent the panch poran from burning. Stir in the turmeric, cayenne and salt. Sauté the masala for 5 minutes, or until the oil glistens on the tomatoes. Pour in the water and stir to combine. Add the cream, stir well and cook the curry until it comes to a boil. Reduce the heat to low and simmer for 5 minutes, or until little droplets of oil glisten on top. Serve hot. Will keep refrigerated in an airtight container for up to 1 week.

PANEER

¼ cup white vinegar

½ cup water

1 teaspoon sugar

8 cups whole milk (organic is best)

Paneer is a very popular mild Indian cheese made from whole milk. The most intimidating part of making paneer the first time is (1) setting the heat high enough to boil the milk but not so high as to burn it and (2) allowing the boiling milk to foam almost to the top of the pot and then swirling in the vinegar. This step takes all of five seconds, but if you don't let the milk foam up and rise, you won't get any paneer.

In our super-busy kitchen where every burner is often on simultaneously, we've tried lots of tricks to speed up the boiling yet keep the milk from burning on the bottom of the pot. Our current solution is to combine 1 teaspoon of sugar with ½ cup water and pour this mixture into the pan before adding the milk. There is no actual science that we know of behind the sugar idea, but the Vij's kitchen staff swear by it.

Paneer is very versatile because it does not melt when cooked and it tastes good with just about any vegetable dish or in any rice pilaf. Paneer is frequently added to curries, including such popular ones as paneer and peas, and the queen bee of northern Indian dishes, Saag (page 114). We highly recommend that you try adding paneer to just about any of the vegetarian dishes in this book, or using it in place of any of the vegetables in those recipes.

In India, paneer is considered a staple food in homes that can afford it. (Among the poor, any milk that families can buy is reserved for drinking.) In North America, you can buy packaged paneer from most South Asian grocers, but the homemade version tastes so much better, and making it yourself allows you to adjust the firmness to your liking. The key to making paneer is a heavy-bottomed pot and a good paneer cloth. We use thin white cotton muslin cloths that are sold as tea towels or "flour cloths" or "flour sack towels" online and at many housewares and grocery stores. If you can find the larger, 28-square-inch size, buy those. Otherwise the rectangular ones are fine, as long as they are 26 inches long and at least 18 inches wide. We keep a designated cloth for making paneer and we ensure it is scrupulously clean. First we wash it by hand in the kitchen sink and then we put it in the washing machine, being sure to use only unscented detergent.

HAVE READY an 18- × 26-inch (or larger) cotton muslin paneer cloth. Measure the vinegar into a measuring cup and set aside.

In a small bowl, combine the water and sugar and stir until the sugar dissolves. Pour the mixture into a heavy-bottomed pot large enough to contain the milk and still have 5 inches free at the top. (That's the space for the milk to foam up when it starts to boil.) Pour in the milk and heat on medium-high until it starts to boil and rise, anywhere from 20 to 35 minutes, depending on your stove. (If you smell milk burning at any point, immediately reduce the heat slightly.) As the milk nears the boiling point, be ready with the vinegar in hand. Once the milk has risen about 3 inches (in 3 to 5 seconds), immediately turn off the heat (if you have an electric stove, remove the pot from the element) and drizzle in the vinegar but do not stir. The milk will immediately begin to fall. Without stirring, allow the milk to stand for 15 minutes so the milk solids (the curds) can separate from the liquid (the whey).

Line a colander with the paneer cloth and place it over the sink. Carefully pour the contents of the paneer pot into the colander and allow it to sit for 15 minutes to drain the excess liquid. Gather the four corners of the cloth, bring them together above the paneer, ensuring the milk solids are fairly tightly enclosed inside, and tie the ends together. Fill the pot you boiled the milk in with ½ to ¾ gallon of water. Set the cloth-wrapped paneer in the sink (or on the counter right next to the sink, as there may be leakage) and place the pot of water on top of the milk solids. Gently push down to flatten the paneer and make a stable resting place for the pot. For softer paneer, allow the pot to sit for 15 minutes; for firmer paneer, leave it for up to 45 minutes.

Remove and empty the pot and unwrap the paneer. Set aside the paneer cloth to launder and reuse with your next batch. Transfer the paneer to a clean plate and cover it with plastic wrap (or cut it into cubes and place them in an airtight container). Will keep refrigerated, covered with plastic wrap or in an airtight container, for up to 1 week.

SPICED PUMPKIN SEEDS

2 tablespoons coconut oil or
canola oil

2 cups raw shelled pumpkin seeds

2 tablespoons ground cumin

1 tablespoon sugar

2 teaspoons salt

½ teaspoon ground cayenne
pepper (optional)

2 teaspoons mango powder
(break up any clumps)

Indians believe very strongly that nuts and seeds are important for the health of our bodies and skin. Both contain healthy oils that moisturize the inside of our bodies as well as our skin, and vitamins and minerals that maintain optimal health as well as heal our bodies. Seeds are considered to have more cooling properties than nuts, which become too warm for the body if overeaten. After a woman has given birth, she is fed a mixture of various nuts and seeds cooked in ghee and raw sugar to give her back her strength and to produce breast milk.

We always keep lightly roasted pumpkin and sunflower seeds on hand, as well as spiced nuts. However, Nanaki is allergic to most nuts, so Meeru is always trying to work various seeds (sesame, sunflower, flax or pumpkin) into her diet. What we are learning is that all the mother, aunt and grandmother food lore we grew up with actually has scientific merit. For example, our moms told us that pumpkin seeds are "warmer" than sunflower seeds and that Nanaki should eat more pumpkin, while Shanik should eat more of the "cooler" sunflower. It turns out they were right. Nanaki was a very skinny and constipated child with asthma and easily prone to getting sick, for which pumpkin seeds, high in omega fats and magnesium, are an excellent supplement. Shanik has extremely dry skin and loses her pigmentation in small patches all over body during the winter. A naturopath once recommended vitamin B5 for her pigmentation loss, and sunflower seeds contain a high amount of this.

We sell these spiced pumpkin seeds at Rangoli Market, but you can make the same recipe at home with sunflower seeds, almonds or cashews instead (but note that sunflower seeds will take only 6 to 8 minutes to brown). We use coconut oil in the summer months when it's warm indoors (75°F plus) and canola oil in the winter months, since coconut oil solidifies when cold. Sprinkle these healthy seeds over any dish. As with most Indian foods, you'll notice the delicious flavour before realizing just how healthy these are.

MAKES 2 CUPS
PREP & COOKING TIME: 15 TO 20 MINUTES

HEAT THE OIL in a heavy-bottomed frying pan on medium heat for 1 minute. Add the pumpkin seeds, reduce the heat to medium-low and sauté for 10 minutes, stirring regularly. You will notice the edges turn brown. Stir in the cumin, sugar, salt and cayenne; sauté and stir for 4 minutes. (If the spices are turning dark brown too quickly, immediately remove the pan from the heat.)

Transfer the spiced seeds to a medium bowl, and while they are still very hot, stir in the mango powder. Allow the seeds to cool completely in the bowl. Will keep in an airtight container at room temperature for up to 6 weeks. (You can keep them longer but the spices may begin to lose their zest.)

SPROUTED LENTILS

1 cup mung beans
2 cups cold water

We sprout mung beans (which in India we refer to as mung lentils or *daal*) both at home and at our restaurants. We also sprout black urad lentils and black chickpeas at our restaurants, but these two take twice as much time to sprout as mung beans. The nutritional value of raw sprouted lentils is immense, with lots of vitamins (including B and K) and iron.

Meeru, Shanik and Nanaki sprinkle sprouted lentils on just about everything savoury, even many non-Indian dishes. Vikram prefers the crunch and loves his sprouted lentils with a bit of black salt, chopped ginger, cilantro and lemon as a pre-dinner salad with his cocktail. And although this is not an Indian dish, Shanik and Meeru like to spread avocado on thick slices of hearty bread and top that with as many mung sprouts as possible. We add a dash of salt and pepper and some sauerkraut (Shanik) or kimchee (Meeru).

Like making yogurt at home, sprouting mung beans is much simpler than most people think. All we do is leave the mung beans in a bowl of water on our kitchen counter and rinse them with fresh water every ten to twelve hours. They take forty-eight hours to sprout completely at room temperature, or up to sixty hours in a cool room. Nanaki sprouts mung beans regularly in her dorm room at McGill (and sends us photos because she never ceases to be amazed at how "cool" it is—and how easy they are to eat once sprouted). Give them a try!

At our restaurants we steam all of our sprouted lentils as a food-safety precaution. However, at home, in all of our years of sprouting lentils, we have never steamed them.

MAKES 2 ½ CUPS

PREP TIME: 5 MINUTES TO ASSEMBLE + 2 TO 3 DAYS TO SPROUT

HAVE READY a 4-cup glass or stainless steel bowl with a fitted lid. Place the mung beans in a medium bowl and run them under cold water. Drain well. Repeat this rinsing and draining once more. Pour the beans into the lidded bowl, add the 2 cups of water, cover and allow to sit on the counter at room temperature for 10 to 12 hours.

Wash your hands thoroughly to remove any bacteria, then remove the lid and carefully pour out the water. Add 1 to 1 ½ cups fresh cold water, cover with the lid again and return to the counter for another 10 to 12 hours.

This time, when you carefully pour out the water, you will notice that the lentils have sprouted significantly. Again, add 1 to 1 ½ cups fresh water, replace the cover and allow to sit on the counter for another 10 to 12 hours. Continue this process of draining and refreshing the water for 48 hours.

After 48 hours, spoon a few of the sprouts into your mouth to see if they are soft enough for you. They will be crunchy, but if you prefer them less crunchy, refresh the water and allow the lentils to sprout for another 10 to 12 hours. You can keep going with this refreshing and sprouting routine for up to 3 days, until the lentils have softened to your liking.

Before storing your sprouted lentils, pour off all the water. Will keep refrigerated in an airtight container for up to 1 week.

CANDIED FENNEL AND INDIAN THYME WALNUTS

½ teaspoon butter

1 ½ teaspoons ghee or butter

½ teaspoon fennel seeds

¼ teaspoon ajwain (Indian thyme) seeds

½ cup raw sugar

½ teaspoon salt

¼ teaspoon ground cayenne pepper

1 cup raw walnut halves

These candied walnuts are perfect as snacks with drinks or at the end of a meal with dessert wine or cognac. At Vij's, we have also used these walnuts in many dishes—in particular, we've combined them with the Roasted Spicy Okra (page 94) as a topping for the Mildly Curried Beef Short Ribs (page 211). We also use them to top off our Beet Bites (page 51) because they add a crunchy texture and sweetness.

This recipe does require a certain comfort level with heating sugar and cooking it quickly while gauging the heat of your stove. If you need to, add an extra ½ teaspoon of ghee or butter while cooking the walnuts in the sugar so the sugar doesn't burn and the mixture is easier to stir.

MAKES 1 ¼ CUPS

PREP & COOKING TIME: 30 MINUTES

ON A SMALL baking sheet or in a baking dish, lightly grease a circle about 8 inches in diameter using the ½ teaspoon of butter. Set aside.

Melt the 1 ½ teaspoons of ghee (or butter) in a medium, heavy-bottomed pot on medium heat. Add the fennel and ajwain seeds and allow them to sizzle gently for 1 minute. Reduce the heat to low and add the raw sugar, salt and cayenne, stirring regularly until the sugar melts, about 3 minutes. Stir in the walnuts, using a firm hand to ensure the nuts are well mixed into the sticky melted sugar. Stir and cook the walnuts for 2 minutes. The sugar will darken and some of it will stick to the bottom of the pan. This is fine, but if the sugar begins to burn, remove the pot from the heat before continuing to stir the walnuts.

Immediately scrape the mixture (be sure to get all the fennel and ajwain seeds) onto the buttered baking sheet (or dish), doing your best to spread the thick and sticky walnuts into a single layer. (A rubber spatula is best for this.) Don't be afraid to use some firm force when spreading. Allow the mixture to cool for 10 minutes.

Using a large knife, break the walnuts into bite-sized pieces. You may need to transfer the hardened nut mixture to a chopping board first. Will keep in an airtight container at room temperature for up to 10 days.

CHAI WITH VARIATIONS

In general, *chai* means "tea with milk," and it is a staple in every Indian home. So it's not possible to write a Vij's cookbook without offering a chai recipe to serve at any time of the day. In addition to the version we have been serving our customers for more than twenty years, here we give you two recipes from our kitchen staff as well. The Punjabi chai is much like a latte, with less caffeine but more sugar than our Vij's chai; this is the chai that some children will drink before school, since it is full of milk. The black cardamom and ginger chai is perfect in cold months because it is soothing and helps to prevent colds—it has a slightly smoky flavour from the black cardamom and a spiciness from the ginger.

The key to Indian chai is to serve it piping hot. Since we vigorously boil the tea leaves or bags, we do not use the more delicate and expensive teas. We also do not use cinnamon in our chai. In fact, we can't recall ever having Indian chai made with cinnamon in any Indian home. "Chai" with no specifications means tea with milk and sugar. Unless you are making Punjabi chai, the sugar and milk are optional.

MAKES 6 CUPS (EACH RECIPE)
PREP & COOKING TIME: 20 TO 30 MINUTES

VIJ'S CHAI Set a small bowl and tea strainer/sieve beside the stove before you begin. In a kettle or pot, combine the water, cardamom pods and fennel seeds and bring to a vigorous boil on high heat. Reduce the heat to medium-low and allow to boil for another 2 minutes. Add the teabags and sugar, stir well and allow to boil for 1 to 1 ½ minutes more, or longer if you like a stronger-flavoured tea.

Using the sieve or a large spoon, remove the teabags and place in the bowl. Add the milk to the pot and continue to heat through for 45 seconds to 1 minute (you don't want the milk to boil over). Turn off the heat. Place the tea strainer over the mouth of a teapot and pour the chai into it. Or hold the strainer over individual cups before pouring. Serve immediately.

VIJ'S CHAI

5 ½ cups water

12 to 15 green cardamom pods, lightly crushed

½ tablespoon fennel seeds

5 orange pekoe teabags

6 teaspoons sugar (optional)

¾ cup whole milk (optional)

PUNJABI CHAI

1 ½ cups water

12 to 15 green cardamom pods, lightly crushed

½ tablespoon fennel seeds

3 orange pekoe teabags

5 cups whole milk

8 teaspoons sugar

BLACK CARDAMOM AND GINGER CHAI

6 cups water

2 black cardamom pods (with moist black seeds), lightly crushed

1 tablespoon roughly chopped unpeeled ginger

5 orange pekoe teabags

6 teaspoons sugar (optional)

¾ cup whole milk (optional)

continued...

PUNJABI CHAI Have ready a tall and narrow pot for this chai. Set a small bowl and tea strainer/sieve beside the stove before you begin. In the narrow pot, combine 1 cup of the water, the cardamom pods, fennel seeds and teabags; bring to a boil on high heat. Stir, reduce the heat to low and allow to simmer for 5 to 7 minutes.

Using the sieve or a large spoon, remove the teabags and place in the bowl. Add the milk and sugar to the pot, increase the heat to medium and bring the chai just to the boiling point. Because the tea is so milky, we prefer to pour Punjabi chai directly into individual cups. Hold the strainer over the cups before pouring. Serve immediately.

BLACK CARDAMOM AND GINGER Set a small bowl and tea strainer/sieve beside the stove before you begin. In a kettle or pot, combine the water, cardamom pods and ginger; bring to a boil on high heat. Reduce the heat to low, cover and simmer for 10 minutes. Add the teabags and sugar, stir well and allow to boil for 1 to 1 ½ minutes more, or longer if you like a stronger-flavoured tea.

Using the sieve or a large spoon, remove the teabags and place them in the bowl. Increase the heat to medium, add the milk to the pot and heat through for 45 seconds to 1 minute. Turn off the heat. Place the tea strainer over the mouth of a teapot and pour the chai into it. Or hold the strainer over individual cups before pouring. Serve immediately.

SNACKS

AND

STARTERS

EATING, THE INDIAN WAY

The concept of different courses in a meal—appetizer, main course, dessert—is a Western one. In India, all the dishes in a meal are served in family-style bowls and platters at the table so that guests can help themselves to what they want all at once or as they want it. A typical dinner includes small, simple, rich and extravagant dishes. The general rule is that if any food requires a plate and/or bowl and a spoon, then it is meant for dinner. If you can eat it with your hands, then it can be served before dinner as an hors d'oeuvre. At Vij's, we serve complimentary hors d'oeuvres to our customers who are waiting for a table. These particular dishes tend to be easy to prep and pass around in a crowded room where many people are standing.

A few years ago, we decided that we wanted to serve more sophisticated and creative hors d'oeuvres at Vij's, dishes that people could share at the table rather than in our lounge before sitting down to their main course. So we added some bite-sized servings to our appetizer menu. Every dish in this section is meant to be shared and eaten before dinner. All of them can also be served as the perfect Indian complement to a non-Indian dinner party. Most are visually stunning and unusually bold in their flavours and combination of ingredients.

BEET BITES

These bites were inspired by a conversation Vikram and Meeru had over dinner one night. We'd been working together all day and we were bored with each other's company. Meeru asked Vikram who he'd rather be eating dinner with at that moment, and he replied, "Nusrat Fateh Ali Khan" (a Pakistani musician who is now deceased). Meeru responded that she'd like to have dinner with Jónsi (the lead singer of the Icelandic band Sigur Rós). When we looked at photos of both musicians, we roared with laughter at how chunky and meat-eating one of them looked and how thin and vegetable-eating the other appeared. It turned out that Jónsi is a raw food vegan. Vikram teased, "I don't think that even you could muster up an entire raw food vegan dinner. Besides, your mouth would get so tired chewing all that raw food, you wouldn't have any energy left to talk, which would be torture for you." An entire raw food dinner? No, Meeru thought. But just one raw food vegan dish, in honour of Jónsi, was in order.

When Meeru first served these beet bites to the family, she topped them with raw pecans (one of the few nuts Nanaki is not allergic to). To the embarrassment of her daughters, she played Sigur Rós music loudly while she explained details of the layers of flavours everyone was tasting as they ate. She even tried to get everyone to eat according to the pace of the music! When Nanaki had finished eating, she said, "Mom, these beet thingies are really good, but don't ever think that what you did with all that explanation and the music was cool. Just serve them at Vij's." Which we did.

Here in the Pacific Northwest, beets are abundant from early summer to early winter—we have purple/red beets, golden beets, red-and-white Chioggia beets. You can use any beet in this recipe, but we prefer the deep red ones for their colour. (And if you use those, remember to wear rubber gloves when preparing this dish, so you don't have red stains on your hands for the rest of the day!) The most important thing to remember is to chop your ingredients very finely, because you don't want anyone to bite into a big piece of raw garlic, ginger or jalapeño pepper. Stick to the amounts we've suggested here, except that you may need to

1 ½ pounds raw beets

⅓ cup very finely chopped cilantro

1 ½ tablespoons chickpea flour

1 tablespoon very finely chopped garlic (3 to 4 medium cloves)

1 tablespoon very finely chopped ginger

1 teaspoon finely chopped jalapeño pepper

1 teaspoon ground black pepper

1 teaspoon salt

continued...

use less or more jalapeño, depending on how hot your particular pepper is. One teaspoon is based on a very hot pepper. And don't skip the chickpea flour, as it not only helps bind the beets but provides a hint of nutty flavour.

If you're in a hurry or wanting a purely raw vegan dish, you can make these bite-sized balls and serve them on their own, topped with raw nuts. But adding all the bells and whistles to each bite—a dollop of the Sour Cream Dressing (page 27) and a ½-inch piece of the Candied Fennel and Indian Thyme Walnuts (page 44)—will give you a truly elegant starter with several layers of flavour and texture.

SERVES 10 (MAKES 30 BITE-SIZED BALLS)
PREP TIME: 1 HOUR

PEEL AND COARSELY grate the beets and place them in a large bowl. Add the cilantro, chickpea flour, garlic, ginger, jalapeños, black pepper and salt. Mix well with both hands.

Have ready a large serving platter or a baking sheet. Working over the sink or a large bowl, scoop about 1 tablespoon of the beet mixture into the palm of your hand and squeeze out the excess water into the sink (or bowl). Roll the mixture between your palms to make a ball. Press it slightly flat on the bottom and set your beet bite, flat side down, on the platter(or baking sheet) so it doesn't roll around. Repeat with the remaining beet mixture. (You should have about 30 bites.) You can serve the beet bites immediately or chill them, covered, in the fridge for a few hours. Will keep refrigerated in an airtight container for up to 2 days, after which they begin to release their liquid and become mushy.

TO SERVE Pass around the platter of beet bites.

SWEET POTATO AND RICOTTA "COOKIES"

2 pounds sweet potatoes, peeled

1 teaspoon mild ancho chili powder

1 teaspoon ground cayenne pepper

1 teaspoon salt

½ cup + 1 tablespoon cooking oil

1 tablespoon finely chopped garlic (3 to 4 medium cloves)

1 teaspoon ground cumin

½ teaspoon dried green fenugreek leaves

8 ounces full-fat ricotta cheese

At Vij's, we offer these ricotta-filled "cookies" with curried chickpeas as an appetizer on our menu, but on their own they make a great snack to pass around at any time of the day. Just pick them up and eat them like cookies. They go well with all sorts of drinks—from beer to sparkling wine to a rich red wine. However, do not serve these cookies with milk!

Although we do a lot of cooking at home, we never make baked desserts. So when Shanik saw these on the counter one day before a dinner party, she was surprised and said: "Oh! Those are funny-looking cookies. Are they for dessert?" Vikram teased that they were the closest Meeru would ever get to making homemade cookies.

Use only sweet potatoes in this recipe because you want their texture—do not substitute yams or regular potatoes. Save the trimmed ends of the sweet potatoes for another recipe or just make tiny cookies with them instead.

If you make these filled cookies ahead of time and need to reheat them, arrange them on a baking sheet and warm them in a preheated 300°F oven (or toaster oven) for 3 to 5 minutes.

SERVES 6 (2 COOKIES PER PERSON)
PREP & COOKING TIME: 45 MINUTES

USING A SHARP knife, cut the sweet potatoes into 24 rounds, each ¼ inch thick. Place the rounds in a large bowl and add the ancho chili powder, ½ teaspoon of cayenne, ½ teaspoon of salt and ¼ cup of the oil. Toss until potato rounds are evenly covered with oil and spices. Set aside.

To make the filling, heat the 1 tablespoon of oil in a small pot on medium heat. Add the garlic and sauté for 2 minutes, or until golden. Stir in the cumin and turn off the heat. Add the remaining ½ teaspoon of cayenne, ½ teaspoon of salt and all of the fenugreek leaves; stir well. Allow the mixture to cool for 5 minutes. Add the ricotta and stir to mix well. Set aside.

Line a baking sheet with paper towels. In a heavy-bottomed frying pan large enough to hold 4 sweet potato rounds, heat

1 teaspoon of the oil (you will need about 1 teaspoon for every 4 rounds) on high heat for 2 minutes. Reduce the heat to medium-high and add 4 sweet potatoes—in a single layer—to the pan. Cook on one side for 2 minutes. Using a pair of tongs or a spatula, turn the sweet potatoes over and cook them for 1 minute more. If they are tender, remove them from the heat. If not, cook them for 1 minute more. Add more oil if they begin to stick or burn. Transfer the cooked rounds to the paper towel–lined baking sheet and allow to cool for 5 minutes before filling. Add 1 teaspoon oil to the pan and cook the next batch of sweet potatoes while the first ones are cooling.

To fill the cookies, choose 2 sweet potato rounds of similar size. Spoon 1 teaspoon of the ricotta filling onto one of the rounds. Place the other sweet potato round on top to form a sandwich "cookie." Fill the remaining rounds until you have 24 cookies. Serve hot or warm. Leftover cookies will keep refrigerated in an airtight container for up to 5 days.

TO SERVE Arrange the cookies on a platter and pass them around.

PANI-PURI (GOL GUPPA) WITH SHRIMP CEVICHE

PANI

6 cups cold water

15 to 20 fresh mint leaves, chopped as finely as possible

3 tablespoons Tamarind Paste (page 26)

3 tablespoons white sugar

1 tablespoon ground cumin

2 teaspoons salt OR 1 teaspoon salt + 1 teaspoon black salt

SHRIMP CEVICHE FILLING

1 pound raw shrimp, cut into bite-sized pieces

½ cup fresh lemon juice

1 to 2 sprigs cilantro, very finely chopped

1 teaspoon salt

½ teaspoon ground cayenne pepper

CHICKPEA AND/OR POTATO FILLING

2 cups cooked or drained canned chickpeas OR 2 pounds of your favourite potatoes, boiled, peeled and finely diced

1 teaspoon salt

1 teaspoon finely ground coriander (optional)

½ teaspoon ground cayenne pepper

1 to 2 sprigs cilantro, very finely chopped

In northern India, pani-puri is also known as *gol guppa*. In our opinion, pani-puri should win the prize for most original and satisfying snack in the world. *Pani* refers to the spiced sweet-tart water you pour into the puri, which is the bite-sized deep-fried chapatti, or flatbread, that holds it. To prepare a pani-puri, you poke a hole in the top of the deep-fried chapatti and fill the hole with a teaspoon of food and a teaspoon or two of the water. Then you pop the whole thing into your mouth, bite down and revel in the explosion of textures and flavours.

On weekends in the summer, we love to invite friends over for a relaxing all-day party on our deck, and these are by far our favourite snack. We place a big bowl of the puri in the middle of the table with a pitcher of pani on the side. In separate serving bowls with teaspoons, we'll put spiced chickpeas and spiced boiled and diced potatoes. Everyone just serves themselves, adding as much or as little filling as they like to their little puris. By seven in the evening, someone will add vodka to the remaining pani and we suddenly have cocktails! Vikram also serves these snacks at My Shanti, where he uses shrimp ceviche in place of the traditional chickpeas and presents the pani in little shot glasses. It's the top-selling appetizer at that restaurant, and the beautiful street food presentation would make any Indian proud.

Here we give you the recipe for both fillings. Note that for the vegetarian filling, the measurements are for chickpeas *or* potatoes. If you want to make both, make them separately, using the same recipe.

It's far too time-consuming and messy to make the little puris at home, but you can buy very high quality ones cheaply at any Indian food store, so go ahead and purchase them. They are usually sold in resealable bags, and are often locally made if your city has a significant South Asian population—they may not even have a label. The number of puris you buy will determine the number of bite-sized servings you'll be able to make—count on roughly ten per person. If you have pani left over, refrigerate it in a pitcher for up to a week.

PANI In a large pitcher or bowl, combine the water, mint, tamarind paste, sugar, cumin and salt. Stir with a spoon until the ingredients are very well mixed and the sugar and tamarind are completely dissolved. (As you are serving the pani, you will have to stir occasionally to blend the spices and mint that may have fallen to the bottom of the pitcher.) Refrigerate until you are ready to serve.

SHRIMP CEVICHE FILLING Place the shrimp, lemon juice, cilantro, salt and cayenne in a large serving bowl. Stir gently to combine, cover and refrigerate for 3 to 6 hours to allow the flavours to meld before serving.

CHICKPEA AND/OR POTATO FILLING Place the chickpeas (or potatoes), salt, coriander, cayenne and cilantro in a large serving bowl. Mix well.

TO SERVE Set out your fillings in big bowls, family style, your pani in the pitcher and your puris in another large serving bowl. Set out small plates or bowls for your guests along with lots of teaspoons for filling the puris. Or skip the small plates and encourage everyone to fill their puris and pop them straight into their mouth! Just keep napkins on hand.

PURÉED LENTIL CURRY SPREAD

½ cup washed, split urad lentils

⅓ cup cooking oil

¼ cup chopped garlic (9 to 12 medium cloves)

15 to 20 fresh curry leaves (optional)

½ tablespoon salt

1 tablespoon ground yellow mustard seeds

1 teaspoon ground fenugreek seeds

1 teaspoon turmeric

1 teaspoon crushed cayenne pepper

2 cups puréed fresh or canned tomatoes (5 to 6 medium)

4 cups water

1 cup whipping cream (optional)

Years ago, Meeru came up with a recipe for an Indian chicken liver pâté, and it was a big hit on our Vij's menu. Meeru later decided to create a vegetarian pâté which is just as satisfying. Once we put this lentil curry spread on our Vij's menu, it was ordered as much as the chicken liver pâté. Serve this dish as you would hummus, as a dip with slices of baguette, crackers or cut-up vegetables.

You will need a specific lentil called "washed and split urad daal" for this curry, and it's well worth the visit to an Indian grocer to get it.

SERVES 6 TO 8
PREP & COOKING TIME: 45 MINUTES

PLACE THE LENTILS in a spice (or coffee) grinder and grind them until they are similar in texture to fine bulghur wheat or couscous—you do *not* want a fine powder.

Heat the oil in a wok-style frying pan on medium-high heat for 1 minute. Add the garlic and sauté until it is light golden, about 2 minutes. Stir in the ground lentils and cook for 2 to 4 minutes, or until they begin to foam lightly. Add the curry leaves, salt, yellow mustard seeds, fenugreek, turmeric and cayenne. Stir and sauté for 2 minutes. Add the tomatoes and stir well (keeping your face away from the pan, as the liquid from the tomatoes will splatter slightly). Cook the tomatoes, stirring them into the lentil mixture, for 5 minutes, or until the oil glistens on top.

Pour in the water, stir thoroughly and allow the mixture to come to a boil. Reduce the heat to low, cover and simmer for 5 minutes, or until the oil glistens on top of the curry. Gently stir in the whipping cream, increase the heat to medium and bring the curry to a low boil. Reduce the heat to low, cover and simmer for 5 minutes.

TO SERVE Remove and discard the curry leaves. Spoon the curry spread into a bowl and serve family style.

NAPA CABBAGE IN TOMATO MASALA SALAD

The idea for this recipe came to us after we learned how to make kimchee—the spicy Korean side dish made from fermented napa cabbage—with our friend Grace Kim's mom. Now we add kimchee to everything, from Indian curry to Italian pasta, so there is panic in the home if there is no kimchee in the fridge. This raw salad is nowhere near as time-consuming to make as kimchee and is very easy to make with Indian spices. And, like kimchee, it tastes good with everything. You can serve this salad as a starter and keep it at the table as a side throughout dinner.

Napa cabbage is light and refreshing when it's raw, but when cooked too long it wilts away to nothing and releases too much water. To keep its texture for this salad, cook the spices with onion and garlic and then stuff the cabbage. If you want a stronger Indian flavour, add ground cumin. If you prefer a lighter Indian flavour, skip the cumin. Once, we took this salad to dinner at a neighbour's home, and it made a delicious and different combination with her homemade pizza.

SERVES 8 TO 10

PREP & COOKING TIME: 45 MINUTES + 30 MINUTES TO 3 HOURS FOR THE MASALA TO "FALL INTO" THE CABBAGE

HEAT THE OIL in a frying pan on medium-high heat for 1 minute. Add the onions and sauté for 6 to 8 minutes, or until golden brown. Stir in the garlic and sauté for 3 minutes, or until the garlic is golden and the onions are a darker brown. Reduce the heat to medium and add the tomatoes, stirring well to combine them. Add the cumin, coriander, ancho chili powder, cayenne and salt (if using now). Stir and sauté for 5 minutes, or until the oil glistens on the tomatoes and the water has evaporated. Pour the masala into a bowl and set aside until cool enough to touch, about 15 minutes.

Place the napa cabbage, core side down, on a large plate. Using your hands, very gently pull a couple of the outer layers of leaves away from the inner ones, without separating them from the core. You basically want to loosen up the leaves enough to be able to

¼ to ⅓ cup cooking oil

1 cup finely chopped onions (1 medium-large)

1 tablespoon finely chopped garlic (3 to 4 medium cloves)

3 cups chopped fresh tomatoes (about 5 medium)

1 tablespoon ground cumin (optional)

1 tablespoon ground coriander

1 tablespoon mild ancho chili powder

½ teaspoon ground cayenne pepper (optional)

¾ teaspoon salt (or to taste after tossing)

1 head napa cabbage (about 2 ½ pounds)

juice of ½ lemon

continued...

stuff them with tomato masala. Using a spoon or your hands or a combination, and starting close to the core, stuff the masala as deeply between the cabbage leaves as you can, using all the masala. Some of the masala will fall onto the plate, and that is fine. We like to refrigerate the "stuffed" cabbage for a few hours so that the masala can "fall" into it, but you can serve it after chilling for just ½ hour if you're in a hurry.

TO SERVE Place the stuffed cabbage on its side on a cutting board. With a sharp knife, slice the cabbage crosswise into rounds ½ to 1 inch thick. Place the cabbage rounds and all of the masala from the plate in a large salad bowl. Sprinkle with the lemon juice. Do not stir or toss until right before serving. Season to taste with salt (if you didn't add it to the masala). Leftovers will keep for up to 24 hours, but remember that napa cabbage wilts easily.

SAVOURY INDIAN TRUFFLES
(PANEER AND CASHEWS)

1 tablespoon roughly ground raw unsalted cashews

2 tablespoons unsweetened dried ground coconut (do not buy "shredded")

8 ounces soft Paneer (page 38), grated

6 ounces unpeeled new potatoes (2 to 3 whole ones), boiled and grated

⅓ cup finely chopped cilantro

1 tablespoon chickpea flour

1 tablespoon finely chopped ginger

1 teaspoon finely chopped jalapeño pepper

1 teaspoon salt

½ teaspoon ground black pepper

Our family has a tradition of meeting for coffee three to four afternoons a week, at four o'clock. Two or three times a month, for years, we have visited German chocolatier and pastry chef Thomas Haas's Vancouver café for our coffee time. Meeru loves looking at the beautiful displays of white and dark chocolate truffles in his store, and this dish was inspired by those rich and decadent signature chocolates.

These sophisticated savoury and spicy Indian truffles are a nod to Thomas's friendship and skill as a chocolatier—Meeru was tempted to call this dish "I heart Thomas Haas" on her menu. At Vij's, we have served them as a family-style appetizer as well as a vegetarian entrée. As a main, we pair these truffles with the Bengali-style Curry (page 36) and the Zucchini, Squash and Potato Sauté (page 106). For best results, use soft homemade paneer (it should have the texture of a grated mild cheddar cheese) and new potatoes for their superior texture and flavour.

SERVES 12 (2 PER SERVING)
PREP & COOKING TIME: 35 TO 45 MINUTES,
IF YOU'VE ALREADY MADE THE PANEER

HEAT A SMALL, heavy-bottomed frying pan on medium heat for 1 minute. Add the cashews and cook for 1 minute, stirring constantly. Add the coconut and cook for another minute, stirring constantly. You will see the coconut turn brown (but do not let it become dark brown). Immediately transfer this mixture to a small shallow bowl or a plate to prevent it from burning in the pan. Set aside.

In a large bowl, combine the grated paneer and potatoes, cilantro, chickpea flour, ginger, jalapeños, salt and black pepper; mix well. Taste a small amount to check for flavour and adjust the balance of heat from the jalapeño with the cilantro and ginger to suit your preference. Season to taste with more salt and pepper, if needed.

Have ready a large serving platter or a baking sheet. Spoon 1 level tablespoon of the paneer mixture into your hand. Roll it between your palms until you have a ball about 1 ½ inches in diameter (slightly smaller is fine too). Press it slightly flat on the bottom and set your truffle, flat side down, on the platter (or baking sheet) so it doesn't roll around. Repeat with the remaining paneer mixture. (You should have about 24 balls.)

Gently roll each of the truffles in the cashew-coconut topping and arrange it on the platter (or baking sheet). Serve these immediately at room temperature, or chill them slightly before serving. Will keep refrigerated in an airtight container for up to 5 days.

TO SERVE Pass around the platter of truffles.

PUNJABI HEART ATTACK!

1 tablespoon ghee

⅓ cup packed raw sugar

⅔ cup raw unsalted cashews, chopped into small pieces

½ teaspoon salt

¼ teaspoon ground cayenne pepper

1 cup (6 to 7 ounces) grated Paneer (page 38)

¼ cup whipping cream

This rich appetizer has become one of the signature dishes at Vij's. It's so popular that even when it's not on the menu we get enough requests that we make it. We usually serve small amounts on decorative spoons, but every once in a while we will serve it in tiny bowls. The combination of cream, ghee, cashews and paneer means that a little goes a long way. Make this recipe when you have a cup of paneer left over from making another dish.

The name of this dish is a cheeky reference to our ethnicity and just how much of these ingredients Meeru and the kitchen staff ate while perfecting the recipe. One afternoon, Vikram stopped by the kitchen to find Amarjeet, Sital and Meeru acting slightly ill. When he asked what was wrong, Meeru quipped, "We are having Punjabi heart attacks!" Needless to say, the staff were more than surprised when Meeru put the dish on the menu with this name.

This recipe cooks very quickly on high heat, so have all your ingredients at hand before you begin. Be sure to use Ghee (page 24), as butter will burn.

SERVES 12 (1 TO 1 ½ TABLESPOONS PER SERVING)
PREP & COOKING TIME: 20 MINUTES, IF YOU'VE ALREADY
MADE THE PANEER

HAVE READY 24 decorative tasting spoons (or tiny bowls). Heat the ghee in a small pot on high heat for 30 seconds. Stir in the raw sugar and continue stirring and cooking until the sugar melts completely, 1 to 2 minutes. Add the cashews and continue cooking and stirring for 1 minute. Stir in the salt and cayenne, and then add the paneer and whipping cream. Cook, stirring well, for 1 ½ minutes. Remove from the heat and, stirring constantly, allow to cool for 2 minutes.

TO SERVE Carefully drop a tablespoonful (or slightly more) of the hot paneer mixture into each of the spoons (or bowls). Serve hot (but not piping hot, as very hot sugar and ghee can burn your lips).

BACON-WRAPPED PANEER WITH HONEY-BRANDY DIPPING SAUCE

1 teaspoon fennel seeds

1 cup pure unpasteurized honey (any kind)

2 to 3 tablespoons brandy (or more, to taste)

1 pound thickly sliced bacon

1 tablespoon cumin seeds

8 to 9 ounces Paneer (page 38), cut into ¾-inch cubes

When Vikram and Meeru were growing up in the 1970s, our moms would feed us spoonfuls of warmed honey and brandy whenever we had a cold or flu. Naturally we conked out and woke up feeling better—at least we think we did. Once we hit our teen years, this practice came to a halt. While this "medicine" was meant to relieve our aches and pains and give us a good sleep, we just remember how delicious it tasted. When our vegetarian moms learned of our new recipe, which pairs a variation of that early medicine with *bacon*, they were mortified. If you're not vegetarian, you'll love the combination of creamy paneer, crispy salty bacon and sweet boozy sauce.

The key to making this dish taste great is using high-quality ingredients and knowing how to fry bacon. You need the bacon to be cooked but not so crispy that you can't roll it around the paneer. Buy the best-quality nitrate-free bacon you can; it will taste better. And a thicker cut will ensure that the cooked bacon doesn't crack as you try to wrap it around the paneer. You'll need slices 6 inches long, and you probably won't need an entire pound. Since the honey-brandy sauce is crucial to the final dish, splurge on a pure Grade A or No. 1 unpasteurized honey and a quality brandy.

Wrapping the bacon around the paneer will be much easier while the meat is still warm, so have the paneer cubed before you begin cooking the bacon. Once you prepare and wrap the paneer in bacon, eat it straight away or the bacon will become hard and chewy.

SERVES 12 (2 PER SERVING)

PREP & COOKING TIME: 30 MINUTES, IF YOU'VE ALREADY MADE THE PANEER

HEAT A SMALL, heavy-bottomed saucepan on high heat for 1 minute. Reduce the heat to medium, add the fennel seeds and dry-roast them, gently shaking the pan over the heat until the seeds turn slightly brown, 1 to 2 minutes. Remove the pan from the heat and add the honey. Return the pan to the heat and stir until the honey softens and is hot, but nowhere near boiling. Stir in the brandy. Remove from the heat and set aside.

continued...

Line a large plate with paper towels. Heat a large, heavy-bottomed frying pan on medium-high heat and add as many strips of bacon as will fit in the pan while still allowing you to easily turn the bacon while it is cooking. As soon as the bacon begins to release its fat, sprinkle in a portion of the cumin seeds (use an equal amount per batch). Continue frying the bacon on one side for 2 to 3 minutes, then turn it over and cook the other side for about the same time. Adjust this cooking time according to the thickness of your bacon, as you do not want to overcrisp it. Don't worry that the cumin seeds will burn. They'll be fine as they sizzle along with the bacon. Once the bacon is cooked, transfer it to the paper towel–lined plate to drain. Using a spatula or spoon, scoop the cumin seeds out of the pan and sprinkle them over the bacon. Cook the remaining bacon and cumin seeds.

Have ready a large serving platter. Arrange the cubes of paneer on a clean work surface. While the bacon is still warm and soft, wrap one slice around each cube of paneer. Be sure that there are some cumin seeds on the bacon itself. Arrange the bacon-wrapped paneer on the platter.

When you are ready to serve, stir the honey-brandy over medium-low heat for a few minutes, until it is very warm to the touch.

TO SERVE Serve the platter family style (or serve 2 bacon-wrapped paneer per person on individual plates). Pour the honey-brandy sauce into one or more dipping bowls and serve alongside (or drizzle it over the platter or plates, if you prefer).

PORK BELLY SPOONS

These pork belly spoons are a regular feature on the menu at Vij's, where we serve them with an apple-mint chutney. For dinner parties at home, we serve the pork belly (topped with the cilantro stems) in a large shallow serving bowl along with pieces of baguette or naan to scoop it up. Pork belly is a rich and "porky"-flavoured meat, and if you love the taste of bacon, you will love this cut. This is the meat version of the Punjabi Heart Attack! (page 64) in that just a little bit gives you an explosion of very rich flavours. But while you automatically stop after two spoons of the Heart Attack, it's easy to keep eating this pork belly. If you remember Sloppy Joe sandwiches, this can also be served as a sophisticated version on grilled or toasted ciabatta or baguette.

This is not a difficult recipe to make, but it does take some time since the pork is braised for a couple of hours before being mixed into the masala. Pork belly is denser than shoulder meat and therefore heavier in texture, but it's very tender when slow-cooked. Since raw pork belly contains a lot of fat, it's hard to know how much actual meat you will get once the fat has rendered. Don't worry if you have slightly less or more than the yield we have given below.

The masala is made with chickpea flour. Vikram thinks that Meeru is trying to sneak a bit of healthy fibre into a rich and fatty dish, but Meeru insists that the chickpea flour adds a subtle layer of nuttiness and smoothes out the different spices. The fibre is just a bonus. The chickpea flour will absorb oil, so don't be tempted to cut back on the amount called for. And watch that you don't overbrown the onions when you sauté them with the spices, as they will brown some more when you add the chickpea flour.

MAKES 24 SPOONS (ABOUT 1 TABLESPOON EACH)

PREP & COOKING TIME: 3 ½ HOURS

BRAISED PORK Preheat the oven to 400°F. (If you are using a foil roasting pan, preheat the oven to 375°F instead.)

Place the pork belly in a large roasting pan or casserole dish and add the curry leaves, cumin seeds, salt, cayenne and water. Cover with a lid or aluminum foil and bake for 2 hours. Remove the pork from the oven, carefully (as it will be very hot) remove the lid and

BRAISED PORK

2 pounds skin-on, boneless pork belly

12 to 16 fresh curry leaves

1 ½ tablespoons cumin seeds

½ tablespoon salt

1 teaspoon ground cayenne pepper

4 cups water

BELLY MASALA

¾ cup cooking oil

1 tablespoon kalonji seeds

2 cups finely chopped onions (1 large)

2 tablespoons ground cumin

2 tablespoons ground coriander

1 tablespoon paprika OR mild ancho chili powder

½ tablespoon ground fenugreek seeds

1 teaspoon turmeric

3 tablespoons chickpea flour

3 tablespoons full-fat sour cream

¼ cup finely chopped cilantro stems, without the leaves (optional)

continued...

check that the meat is cooked. The pork should flake easily when poked with a fork. If it's not cooked, replace the cover and return to the oven for 30 minutes. Once cooked, allow it to cool in its liquid for 45 minutes to an hour.

Wearing rubber gloves, pull off and discard the fat from the belly. You will easily see the difference between the fat and the meat. Be sure to remove the fat that is tucked in between the nice chunks of meat. Place the belly meat on a cutting board and chop it finely. Set aside.

Place a fine-mesh sieve over a medium bowl and strain the braising liquid into the bowl. (You should have about 1 cup of liquid.) Discard the solids in the sieve. Combine the belly meat with the stock in the bowl. Set aside.

BELLY MASALA Heat the oil in a medium to large saucepan on medium-high heat for 1 minute. Add the kalonji seeds and allow them to sizzle for 30 seconds. Stir in the onions and sauté them for 7 to 8 minutes, or until golden.

While the onions are cooking, combine the cumin, coriander, paprika (or ancho chili powder), fenugreek and turmeric in a small bowl. Set aside.

Reduce the heat to medium and stir the chickpea flour into the onions. Stir well, making sure there are no clumps of flour. Continue stirring and cooking the chickpea flour for 2 minutes, or until it darkens and begins to smell nutty. Immediately add the combined spices, stir well and cook for an additional minute. Remove from the heat and stir in the sour cream.

Add the belly meat to the masala. Add enough of the braising liquid to get a curry thick enough to keep its texture on a spoon. If you have a substantial amount of braising liquid left over, refrigerate it for another use. Leftover pork belly will keep refrigerated in an airtight container for up to 1 week. Reheat it in a small pan on medium heat and serve once it is hot—do not overheat.

TO SERVE Arrange 24 decorative spoons on a serving platter. Scoop 1 tablespoon of the spiced belly onto each spoon. Be sure that there is no juice in the spoon, as you don't want it to spill on anyone's clothes! Top with the chopped cilantro.

FRUIT CHAAT

1 Fuji or other crunchy apple, unpeeled

1 ripe Bartlett pear, unpeeled

1 navel orange (or any type you enjoy), peeled and seeded, if need be

1 cup blueberries OR 1 banana, cut into ½-inch rounds, OR 1 mango, peeled, pitted and cubed

½ cup Date Chutney (page 28) or another sweet chutney

1 teaspoon mango powder (break up any clumps)

1 teaspoon salt (black or regular)

½ teaspoon ground black pepper

½ cup crisped rice cereal (optional)

½ to ¾ cup Spiced Pumpkin Seeds (page 40) (optional)

Chaat is a very common word in our cuisine that is used for a savoury, sweet and sour snack. It also means to lick your plate. In India, it is common to make various chaats at home for a late-afternoon snack with chai. (Chaat and chai are divine together. Chaat and coffee taste disgusting together.) Most people love to go out and eat chaat at street carts. There are as many styles of chaat as there are regional cuisines of India. This fruit chaat, though, is based on the regional cuisine of Nanaki and Shanik! It started as a way to get them to eat fruit. The only difference between this recipe and the one we make at home is that our girls don't like black salt, which we love.

All chaats balance the three main flavours of savoury, sweet and sour. Here our savoury ingredients include the spices (and, in many chaats, the chickpeas and potatoes). Our sweet comes from the fruit (and sometimes sugar). And our sour is the mango powder (in many chaats it is in the form of yogurt, tamarind or lemon). Most chaats are topped with a crunchy ingredient. Here we use regular crisped rice cereal (but mashed-up potato chips are also common).

This chaat is designed to be made with black salt (or a combination of black salt and ground cayenne pepper, which we use at all our restaurants), but it is an acquired taste for many people. Black salt has such a sulphuric smell that we never open a bag of it during service because inevitably one of our customers will complain about the "funny smell" in the room. If you're feeling brave or you know that you like black salt, we highly recommend that you make this recipe with that ingredient because it's the crowning final spice. However, this chaat will still taste good made with regular salt.

There are no strict rules about which fruits to use or how much of any single ingredient. Taste the chaat as you prepare it and adjust your ingredients and quantities as you go. Just be sure you can taste savoury, sweet and sour in the final dish.

SERVES 4

PREP TIME: 20 MINUTES, IF YOU'VE ALREADY MADE THE DATE CHUTNEY

CUT UP the apple, pear and orange into bite-sized pieces and place them in a large serving bowl. Add the blueberries (or bananas or mango) and toss to combine. Gently stir in the chutney, mango powder, salt and black pepper, making sure all the ingredients are well combined. Refrigerate for at least 1 hour before serving.

TO SERVE Serve the chaat in a large bowl or in individual bowls. Sprinkle with crisped rice and/or pumpkin seeds, or serve these in separate side bowls so everyone can add their own.

SPICED SEMOLINA AND ALMOND MASALA ON ORANGE ROUNDS

SPICED SEMOLINA

½ cup cooking oil

½ cup semolina

2 tablespoons sugar

¾ cup water

1 to 2 organic navel oranges, unpeeled, cut into ¼-inch-thick rounds

ALMOND MASALA

⅓ cup cooking oil

2 cups chopped onions (1 large)

2 tablespoons chopped garlic (6 to 7 medium cloves)

1 tablespoon ground black mustard seeds

1 tablespoon ground coriander

½ tablespoon Garam Masala (page 23)

1 teaspoon ground cayenne pepper

1 teaspoon salt

½ cup slivered almonds

The inspiration for our recipes comes from many sources, some of them food related, some not. This one was created in response to a scene in Ruth Ozeki's book *A Tale for the Time Being*. In a nutshell, a teenager is at a beach in Japan with her great-grandmother. This teenager is being bullied at school and neglected by her parents, and she is angry at her life. With her great-grandmother's encouragement, she releases her anger and frustration by fighting with the waves— punching them with all her force and getting punched (or pushed) back. She does this for hours, and by the end she is physically exhausted yet feels the peace within after letting go of her anger and negative energy. Her great-grandmother, who is a Zen Buddhist priest, tells her she has found her inner "supapawa" (superpower). In this dish, the masala represents the sand right where the waves crash down. The rind of the orange represents the feel in your nostrils when getting knocked down by the waves, and the flesh of the orange represents the sweetness of the sunset and finding one's inner superpower.

Even if you haven't read the book, you'll appreciate the flavours of this dish, which is also an unusual take on the traditional chaat that combines savoury, sweet and sour (if you leave on the orange rind) with a crunchy topping. It's a delicious and refreshing dish that is best eaten with a knife and fork but is still Indian and a pre-dinner enjoyment. We use organic oranges in this recipe. Since they are free of pesticides, the peels are very healthy, and we love the astringent yet refreshing taste of the peel with the masala. If you don't enjoy that flavour, you can cut off the rind when you eat this dish. Sprinkle some of the Spiced Pumpkin Seeds (page 40) on top if you like a little extra crunch. Or if you are making a special dinner and like unusual but delicious flavour combinations, sprinkle some Roasted Spicy Okra with Walnuts and Jelly Beans (page 94) on top.

You will need what seems like a lot of oil for cooking the masala, but you can leave much of it in the pot before serving this dish.

SERVES 6

PREP & COOKING TIME: 45 MINUTES

(NOT INCLUDING PUMPKIN SEEDS OR SPICY OKRA)

SPICED SEMOLINA Combine the oil and the semolina in a medium pot. Cook the mixture on medium-high heat, stirring regularly, for 7 to 8 minutes, or until it darkens in colour. Stir in the sugar and water until well mixed and bring to a gentle boil. Reduce the heat to medium and cook, stirring regularly, for 5 minutes. The water will soak into the semolina grains and the oil will glisten on top. Using a spoon, skim off and discard the oil that sits on top of the semolina. Remove from the heat and set aside.

ALMOND MASALA Heat the oil in a medium frying pan on medium-high heat. Add the onions and sauté for 6 to 8 minutes, or until browned. Reduce the heat to medium, stir in the garlic and sauté for 2 to 3 minutes, or until light golden. Add the mustard seeds, coriander, garam masala, cayenne and salt. Stir and cook the masala for 1 to 2 minutes, making sure the spices are well stirred into the onion and garlic mixture. Stir in the almonds and cook for another 2 minutes. Add the cooked semolina and stir well to combine.

TO SERVE Arrange the orange rounds on individual plates and spoon about ¼ cup of the semolina masala on top of each orange.

CHICKPEAS AND KALE IN CARDAMOM AND CLOVE CURRY

In an ode to the frenzy over kale that's going on in North America and the frenzy over chickpeas that's a constant in our home, we present this richly spiced appetizer. It is the most satisfying double dose of these ingredients, but it's not an overdose. At Vij's, we make two different curries and serve one on top of the other. While the main curry is the one in the title, we also prepare a chickpea-kale-onion curry that is more like a pickle topping. We really enjoy the look of confusion followed by amused affirmation when we tell our customers that this appetizer is chickpeas and kale on chickpeas and kale. Our daughters love the cardamom and clove curry, but they find the pickle "too *Indiany* in the way that some Indians like strong Indian food."

If it seems like too much, you can prepare either one of these recipes on its own. The kale and chickpea curry is delicious topped with a fried egg served sunny side up. The pickle goes with just about anything: we once mixed it into plain cooked pasta and another time used it as a topping for vegetable soup. When you dish up the curry and the pickle together, serve it with some hearty bread or plain steamed rice.

Before you make this dish you may need to take a trip to an Asian grocery store to buy some of the spices. The dried cayenne peppers are usually not that spicy when used whole, but they add a smoky flavour and look beautiful. The more you break up each chili, the more heat it will emit, so warn your guests not to actually bite into a chili unless they like spicy hot!

Since both the curry and the pickle use many of the same ingredients, if you're doing both recipes, do all of the chopping and cooking at once. You'll therefore need a total of 2 cups dried chickpeas (or 4 cans cooked ones) and you will need 2 large onions. If you are using dried chickpeas, first rinse and soak them in 8 cups of water for 6 to 8 hours. Then boil them in their remaining soaking water, covered, for 1 hour, or until they are soft. You can either drain the cooked chickpeas or set aside 1 cup of the cooking liquid to add to the cardamom and clove curry if you prefer it slightly soupy. For the pickle you will need completely drained chickpeas. If you have a pressure cooker, cooking the chickpeas will be much faster.

continued...

⅓ cup + 2 tablespoons cooking oil

1 large onion, cut in half length-wise and thinly sliced

10 dried cayenne peppers

4 ounces kale (any type), stems discarded, chopped

1 teaspoon black cardamom seeds (5 to 10 whole pods)

2 tablespoons ground cumin

½ tablespoon salt

1 teaspoon ground cinnamon

½ teaspoon ground cloves

3 tablespoons Tamarind Paste (page 26)

1 cup dried chickpeas, soaked and cooked, OR 2 cans (each 14 ounces) cooked chickpeas, drained and rinsed

1 cup liquid from cooked chickpeas (optional)

This recipe makes twice as much pickle as you'll need, but it's difficult to make any less. Leftover pickle keeps well refrigerated in an airtight container for up to 10 days. It also makes a great gift in a mason jar. Although our daughters don't enjoy it, our grown-up and non-*Indiany* friends can't get enough of it.

SERVES 6
PREP & COOKING TIME: 45 MINUTES ONCE CHICKPEAS ARE
BOILED OR IF USING CANNED

CARDAMOM AND CLOVE CURRY Heat the ⅓ cup of oil in a large pot on high heat. Add the onions and sauté for 5 minutes, or until the edges have turned brown. Add the cayenne peppers, stir well and sauté for 1 minute. Turn off the heat and stir in the kale. (If the kale is wet, keep your face away from the pot, as the water will splatter.) Continue to stir the kale for 2 minutes. It will completely wilt. Scoop the kale mixture into a medium bowl.

Return the pot to the stove, add the 2 tablespoons of oil and heat it on medium-high heat for 1 minute. Stir in the cardamom seeds and allow them to sizzle for 15 seconds. Turn off the heat and wait for 1 minute. Stir in the cumin, salt, cinnamon, cloves and tamarind paste (keeping your face away from the pot, as the tamarind may splatter slightly). Stir well.

Turn on the heat to medium and sauté the tamarind and spices for 1 minute. Stir in the chickpeas and continue cooking for 5 minutes. Stir in the kale. Add the chickpea cooking liquid if you prefer a soupier curry. Cook for another 5 minutes. Serve immediately, or set aside if you are serving it with the pickle.

CHICKPEA-KALE-ONION PICKLE Heat the ⅓ cup of oil in a large pot on high heat. Add the onions and sauté for 5 minutes, or until the edges have turned dark brown. Add the cayenne peppers, stir well and sauté for 1 minute. Turn off the heat and stir in the kale. (If the kale is wet, keep your face away from the pot, as the water will splatter.) Continue to stir the kale for 2 minutes. It will completely wilt. Set aside.

In a small pot, heat the 3 tablespoons of oil on medium-high heat for 1 minute. Add the kalonji seeds and allow them to sizzle for 30 seconds. Turn off the heat and stir in the fennel, mustard seeds, cumin and salt. Stir well for 1 minute. You will see a bit of foaming from the fennel and mustard, which means they have cooked. If there is no foaming and you don't think the spices are cooking, turn on the heat to medium and cook, stirring, for 1 minute.

To the pot with the kale, add the chickpeas, brown sugar, vinegar and the kalonji spice masala. Mix well. With tongs, transfer the kale and chickpeas to an airtight container. Discard the extra oil and any spices remaining in the pot. Refrigerate until cold and serve as a topping. Alternatively, heat on medium just until it is warmed through before serving.

TO SERVE Using a ratio of two parts curry to one part pickle, spoon the warm curry into individual bowls. Top each serving with a dollop of cold or warm pickle.

CHICKPEA-KALE-ONION PICKLE

⅓ cup + 3 tablespoons cooking oil

1 large onion, cut in half lengthwise and thinly sliced

5 dried cayenne peppers, broken in half

4 ounces kale (any type), stems discarded, chopped

1 teaspoon kalonji seeds

1 tablespoon ground fennel seeds

1 tablespoon ground black mustard seeds

1 tablespoon ground cumin

½ tablespoon salt

1 cup dried chickpeas, soaked and cooked, OR 2 cans (each 14 ounces) cooked chickpeas, drained and rinsed

3 firmly packed tablespoons dark brown sugar

1 tablespoon white vinegar

VEGETARIAN DISHES

A VEGETARIAN FOODIE

Our Mahesh uncle is now eighty years old and living in great content and luxury in New Delhi. He has had a sort of big belly since he was in his thirties. He has also been drinking his evening whiskey copiously since his thirties, and whenever we ask him why he doesn't quit, his answer has always been the same: "I'm a happy and loving man, so I have no reason to quit." Quite frankly, Mahesh uncle loves his life of eating well and enjoying his whiskey, his family and the BBC every evening. Exercise is an added "mental stress" that he doesn't want to bother himself with. Mahesh uncle is also the closest Vikram gets to a kindred spirit, if you exchange the whiskey for good red wine. He is Meeru's father's best friend and he has played a big part in raising Meeru.

Meeru's family moved to the United States in 1969, but Mahesh uncle stayed in India. Whenever we go to Delhi, Mahesh uncle's home is our home and different foods from the kitchen never stop coming. The key is that they are only vegetarian foods, as Mahesh uncle does not allow meat in his household. For breakfast, he drinks a litre of homemade yogurt (it must be homemade) mixed with black salt and pepper. He believes that this has given him the "gut armour" that prevents him from getting any illnesses. Lunch is chapatti with lentils and two or three different vegetable dishes, including a paneer dish. It is a feast, and the food is better than that of any Indian vegetarian restaurant anywhere.

Although everyone else eats earlier, for Mahesh uncle, dinner is at ten at night, after he's drunk his whiskey with some salted nuts. Mahesh uncle eats in his king-sized bed, with his meal served on a tray. Several times during his dinner, he pauses and smiles at his food and at whoever is with him. Every generation of family members thoroughly enjoys sitting with Mahesh uncle as he eats his dinner in bed with the TV tuned to the BBC. Meeru's parents will sit with him, Meeru and Vikram or Mahesh uncle's children of the same age sit with him, and Nanaki and Shanik will also sit with him—all because his evening room is full of laughter.

Mahesh uncle has lived in Delhi since the partition year of 1947. He knows every vegetarian street food stall in Old and New Delhi, and he has always made spur-of-the-moment trips to Chandni Chowk or Karol Bagh markets to eat lunch or five o'clock snacks. During our visits to India, Mahesh uncle will say quite randomly as he is in the middle of doing something: "Fine, I will let you force me to go to Chandni Chowk, but as long as you don't tell your aunty."

Each foodstand has its one or two specialties, which the foodstand man prepares fresh as we wait. Our lunch experience isn't complete if Mahesh uncle doesn't micromanage the

cooking. With a big smile, he insists that the foodstand man make our food fresh and piping hot. We order fried potato tikkis or a chaat of potatoes, chutneys and raw onions. Mahesh uncle's favourite is some type of chickpea dish, most often *channa bhatura* (curried chickpeas with a deep-fried naan-like bread). When the food is ready, we stand at the side of the stall, holding our plates in one hand and using the other hand to scoop the hot food into our mouths. This style of eating is not easy for someone who is not practised, and on every visit Meeru borrows Mahesh uncle's handkerchief to wipe her hands, face and clothes. He jokes that Meeru owes him money for ruining his handkerchief because she can't eat street food with proper Indian street manners. Vikram is more practised from his school days in Mumbai and rejoices in this style of eating.

On one of Meeru's visits to Karol Bagh, Mahesh uncle took her to eat *gol guppa*, a bite-sized crispy deep-fried chapatti filled with a cumin-and-tamarind water called *jal jeera*. Although Meeru's mother had made these snacks (also called Pani-puri, page 56) on Saturday afternoons in the U.S., Meeru was concerned that she'd get sick from eating the ones in the Indian market. "Your parents have pampered you too much," exclaimed Mahesh uncle. "Don't you know that some food is worth getting sick over? It is not possible for your mother to make gol guppa as delicious as this one with your clean American water." He proceeded to order six of the snacks for each of us, with the jal jeera, mint chutney and chickpeas. Mahesh uncle was right—they were the best snack Meeru had ever eaten in her life, and she ordered six more. Meeru was also right—she was sick for the next week. As Meeru lay wailing on Mahesh uncle's bed (and watching BBC), Mahesh uncle joked that he had done her a favour because now she could fearlessly eat everything Delhi had to offer!

Some days later, Meeru and Mahesh uncle returned to the market to eat at the same gol guppa stand. While they ate, Mahesh said, "Eating meat will kill you way before any food-stand man in Delhi." During her last visit to Delhi, Meeru told Mahesh uncle that he was the ultimate foodie. He asked her to explain, but then laughed heartily and said: "You Americans have to find a snobby label for everything that should just come naturally to all people. But if it increases my prestige in your eyes, then call me a vegetarian foodie."

Most of our vegetarian recipes can stand alone as the featured dish on your dinner plate, though you can also serve them as an accompaniment to meats. Some of these recipes have the flair of street food, most are original recipes that reflect our taste and health preferences, and all have a creative twist.

EGGPLANT IN THICK YOGURT AND GARLIC CURRY WITH BATTERED FRIED ONIONS

¼ to ⅓ cup cooking oil

3 tablespoons finely chopped garlic (9 to 10 medium cloves)

3 ½ cups puréed fresh or canned tomatoes (7 to 8 medium)

1 tablespoon ground yellow mustard seeds

½ tablespoon turmeric

½ tablespoon salt

1 teaspoon ground fenugreek seeds

1 teaspoon crushed cayenne pepper

½ cup 10% milk fat Greek-style plain yogurt

4 cups water

½ to 1 bunch spinach or rapini, chopped (optional)

Eggplant originated in India thousands of years ago and it's a staple in many Indian dishes; in fact, it is the country's national vegetable. Both Meeru and Vikram grew up eating some form of eggplant curry at least once a week, and today we still eat eggplant often. This particular recipe was created with a nod to Vikram's love of battered and fried foods. We serve a smaller portion as an appetizer at Vij's, where it is our most popular eggplant recipe of all time. Even people who don't like the texture of eggplant thoroughly enjoy this dish, as the crispy batter and deep-frying seem to offset the mushy texture that some people find unappealing.

Use only big, fleshy purple eggplants, rather than the long, thin Japanese eggplants, for this dish. When Meeru was growing up and took responsibility for the family's weekly grocery shopping, her mother taught her the secret of buying perfect light, fleshy eggplants instead of heavy ones that are full of seeds. The trick is to look for an eggplant with an oval "belly button." At the end opposite the stem, you'll see a dimple that we call the belly button. If it's oval as opposed to round, this is the eggplant you want. Also, if you hold the eggplant, the lighter the eggplant, the fewer seeds and more sweet flesh it will have. To this day, Meeru checks the belly buttons of the eggplants being delivered to Vij's and Rangoli to verify the quality of the flesh. And in our experience, the belly button trick has always held true.

Although the onions can be messy to deep-fry, they do add wonders to the final taste and layering of textures.

SERVES 6 (5 TO 6 SLICES OF EGGPLANT PER PERSON)
PREP & COOKING TIME: 1 ¼ HOURS

YOGURT AND GARLIC CURRY Heat the oil in a medium pot on medium-high heat. Add the garlic and sauté for 2 to 3 minutes, or until light golden. Stir in the tomatoes, and then add the mustard seeds, turmeric, salt, fenugreek and cayenne. Sauté the masala for 4 to 5 minutes, or until the oil glistens on top. Turn off the heat.

Place the yogurt in a bowl. Add a few tablespoons of the masala and stir well. (This step prevents the yogurt from splitting when it is mixed into the hot masala.) Add the tempered yogurt to the masala and turn the heat back on to medium-high. Stir and sauté for 3 to 4 minutes, or until the oil glistens again. Pour some of the water into the yogurt bowl and stir to collect all the yogurt and masala still in the container. Add this water plus the remaining water to the pot, stir and bring to a boil. Reduce the heat to low and simmer for 15 minutes. Prepare the onions while the curry is simmering.

BATTERED FRIED ONIONS In a medium bowl, combine the flour, cayenne, salt and eggs; mix well. You will have a thick batter. Gently but thoroughly mix the onions into the batter. The rounds will break into individual rings.

Line a plate or baking sheet with paper towels. Heat the oil in a heavy-bottomed, deep-sided medium pot on high heat for 5 minutes. Drop a small piece of battered onion into the oil. If the onion rises immediately to the surface and starts sizzling, the oil is hot enough. Carefully ladle half of the battered onions into the oil and fry until the batter is crispy and light golden, about 3 minutes. Using a slotted spoon, transfer the onions to the paper towel–lined plate to drain. Repeat with the remaining onions. Set aside while you prepare the eggplant.

BATTERED EGGPLANT In a large bowl, combine the flour, salt, cayenne, turmeric, water and buttermilk; mix well. Gently mix the eggplant rounds into the batter, being careful not to break them.

Line a plate or baking sheet with paper towels. Heat the oil in a frying pan on high heat for 4 minutes. Reduce the heat to medium-high and, without crowding the pan, carefully add the eggplant in a single layer. (You may need to do this in several batches; be sure you have enough room to flip the eggplant over.) Cook on one side for 3 minutes, then turn over and cook the other side for 3 minutes

BATTERED FRIED ONIONS

1 cup all-purpose flour

1 teaspoon ground cayenne pepper

1 teaspoon salt

3 eggs

1 to 1 ½ pounds onions, cut into thin rounds

4 cups cooking oil

BATTERED EGGPLANT

1 ½ cups all-purpose flour

½ tablespoon salt

1 teaspoon ground cayenne pepper

1 teaspoon turmeric

1 ¼ cups water

¾ cup buttermilk

1 ½ pounds eggplant, cut into ¼-inch rounds

½ cup cooking oil

continued...

more. If the eggplant begins to burn, reduce the heat. Using a slotted spoon, transfer the crisped eggplant to the paper towel–lined plate to drain. Repeat with the remaining eggplant.

TO SERVE Bring the curry to a boil on high heat and immediately remove the pot from the stove. Stir in the spinach (or rapini). Arrange 4 or 5 rounds of fried eggplant on individual plates or in shallow bowls. Divide the hot curry among the plates, pouring it over the eggplant. Top with battered fried onions. Serve immediately.

SUGGESTED PAIRINGS
QUINOA AND CAULIFLOWER SALAD (PAGE 130)
"ETHIOPIAN FLAG" BASMATI RICE PILAF, WITH OR WITHOUT
THE LAMB SHANK (PAGE 221)
SIMPLE GRILLED CHICKEN WITH OPTIONAL
SPICE SPRINKLE (PAGE 190)

EGGPLANT, KALE AND CAULIFLOWER CURRY

⅓ cup coconut oil or cooking oil

¼ teaspoon asafoetida

3 cups puréed fresh or canned tomatoes (6 to 7 medium)

1 tablespoon ground cumin

2 teaspoons salt

2 teaspoons ground black mustard seeds

1 teaspoon ground fenugreek seeds

1 teaspoon turmeric

1 teaspoon crushed cayenne pepper

1 pound eggplant, cut into 2-inch pieces

1 small head cauliflower, cut into 2-inch pieces

2 bunches kale, stems discarded, chopped

28 to 30 ounces (2 cans, each 14 or 15 ounces) premium full-fat coconut milk, stirred

2 cups water

SUGGESTED PAIRINGS
MILLET AND BELL PEPPER PILAF, IN PLACE OF RICE (PAGE 144)
BITTER GOURD WITH POTATOES AND ONIONS (PAGE 116)
LAMB LOIN WITH SAUTÉED BELL PEPPERS AND SUNCHOKES (PAGE 216)

This versatile curry can be adapted to whatever vegetables are in season or in your fridge, as long as you use the same weight of ingredients. For example, at Rangoli we make this curry with jackfruit instead of eggplant. At home, though, jackfruit is a bit of a bother because it requires draining and flash deep-frying.

This is also our go-to "vegan allergy curry," in that it is dairy, gluten and nut free and a big hit with all customers. It is also suitable for Jains, a small and respected sect of Hindus who do not eat any foods grown in the ground (onions, garlic and root vegetables). This belief is based on a strict practice of *ahimsa* (compassionate non-violence), which prohibits the killing of any animal and makes considerable efforts not to injure plants that otherwise die once they are pulled from the ground.

Remember to choose the lighter eggplants with oval "belly buttons" (page 84). Cut the eggplant and cauliflower to any size and shape, as long as all the pieces are roughly the same size. Serve this curry over white Basmati rice.

SERVES 6
PREP & COOKING TIME: 45 MINUTES

HEAT THE OIL in a large pot on medium-high heat for 1 minute. Sprinkle in the asafoetida and allow it to sizzle for 5 seconds. Immediately add the tomatoes and stir. Add the cumin, salt, mustard seeds, fenugreek, turmeric and cayenne. Sauté for 5 minutes, or until the oil glistens on top. Stir in the eggplant and continue cooking for 3 to 4 minutes. Stir in the cauliflower and kale and cook for another 3 minutes. Add the coconut milk and water, increase the heat to high and stir well. Bring the curry to a boil, stirring occasionally, then reduce the heat to low, cover and cook for 10 to 12 minutes. Poke the eggplant and cauliflower with a sharp knife to be sure the eggplant is tender and the cauliflower is cooked but not mushy soft. Remove from the heat.

TO SERVE Ladle equal portions of curry into individual bowls, or pour it into a large tureen and serve it family style.

SAUTÉED BRUSSELS SPROUTS SALAD

¼ cup ghee or coconut oil

¼ teaspoon asafoetida (optional)

2 cups diced canned or fresh, juicy tomatoes (5 medium)

1 teaspoon turmeric

1 teaspoon salt (or ½ tablespoon if using the paneer)

½ teaspoon ground black pepper

½ tablespoon finely chopped ginger

1 pound Brussels sprouts, tough cores trimmed, cut in half

7 to 9 ounces Paneer (page 38), cubed (optional)

SUGGESTED PAIRINGS
QUINOA AND CAULIFLOWER SALAD (PAGE 130)
BEEF SHORT RIBS IN KALONJI AND CREAM CURRY (PAGE 208)
COCONUT JAPANESE-INDIAN GREEN BEAN CURRY, WITH PLAIN BASMATI RICE ON THE SIDE (PAGE 98)

Brussels sprouts are an acquired taste: Meeru loves them; Vikram, Nanaki and Shanik do not. However, Meeru is adamant enough in her love for this vegetable that we always have some form of Brussels sprouts on the fall menu at Vij's. They are surprisingly popular with our customers, especially when we pair this dish with the Quinoa and Cauliflower Salad (page 130). We also serve it as a side salad with many of our lentil, bean and meat dishes.

You may need to play around with the sautéing time until you get the right texture. If you overcook Brussels sprouts, they become bitter yet tasteless. Left too raw, they are also bitter, but with an aftertaste like gasoline. Sautéing the Brussels sprouts in a little ghee with turmeric and ginger brings a beautiful shine to their tender leaves and a simple accent to their natural flavour.

SERVES 6 AS A SIDE SALAD
PREP & COOKING TIME: 30 MINUTES

HEAT THE GHEE (or coconut oil) in a large frying pan on high heat for 1 minute. Sprinkle in the asafoetida and allow it to sizzle for 5 seconds. Immediately add the tomatoes and stir. Add the turmeric, salt, black pepper and ginger; sauté for 3 to 4 minutes, or until tiny beads of oil begin to glisten. (You do not need to thoroughly cook through your masala because turmeric is the only spice; the asafoetida is already cooked.) Stir in the Brussels sprouts, reduce the heat to medium and cook, stirring regularly, for 15 minutes. Add the paneer (if using) and stir gently but thoroughly to combine. Poke a knife into the Brussels sprouts to check that they are cooked to perfection—not too crunchy or mushy. You may need to cook them for an extra few minutes.

TO SERVE Serve family style in a large bowl or platter.

VIJ'S MONARCH BUTTERFLY

This dish is Meeru's ode to the monarch butterfly. Every year for millennia, hundreds of millions of these butterflies have migrated from Canada, down through the United States to either California or Mexico. What is amazing, besides the sheer beauty of watching their delicate orange-and-black wings fluttering as they follow milkweed pathways to their destination, is that the monarchs know exactly where to go, even though they've never been there before. In recent years, however, the population has gone from almost a billion to just three million butterflies, the result of urban development, industrial farms, and pesticides that have killed the milkweed.

While family and staff initially questioned the wisdom of calling a dish on the menu Vij's Monarch Butterfly, Meeru wanted to be as dramatic as possible with this dish, to encourage conversations about butterflies and bees. She explained the name to the front-of-house staff during our daily "chai chat" before the evening service, and they were so excited to talk with customers about this new dish that it has become a top-selling appetizer at Vij's—for its taste as much as for its title.

In addition to the colours in this dish—the orange squashes (acorn, butternut and Marina di Chioggia), red saffron, deep orange tomato masala, black wood ear mushrooms and kalonji seeds—the slightly crispy wood ears represent the cold of Canada while the warm coconut-saffron curry represents the heat of Mexico. This dish is served on deep blue plates to represent the backdrop of the sky.

Look for wood ear mushrooms at most Asian food stores, where they are sold dried. Be sure to choose black ones, rather than brown. Similarly, use mostly red saffron threads. Saffron that is mostly orange is cheaper, but it has very little flavour or colour. Soak the mushrooms and the saffron while you prepare the squash. Ghee is optional, but it adds a lovely caramelized butter flavour. Serve this dish over plain steamed rice.

SERVES 6

PREP & COOKING TIME: 1 ½ HOURS

(INCLUDING THE 30 MINUTES SOAKING TIME)

SQUASH AND WOOD EAR MUSHROOMS

¼ to ⅓ cup cooking oil

6 whole cloves

2 tablespoons demerara sugar

1 teaspoon kalonji seeds

½ teaspoon salt

1 ½ pounds orange-fleshed winter squash, unpeeled, halved and cut into ⅛-inch slices

2 to 2 ½ ounces dried wood ear mushrooms

3 cups very hot tap water

SAFFRON CURRY

½ teaspoon (2 pinches) saffron threads

½ cup very hot tap water

1 ½ to 2 tablespoons ghee, butter or cooking oil

2 teaspoons cumin seeds

1 teaspoon turmeric

1 teaspoon ground cayenne pepper

1 teaspoon salt

2 cups premium full-fat coconut milk, stirred

¾ cup water

TOMATO MASALA

1 tablespoon cooking oil

¾ cup crushed or ground canned tomatoes

1 tablespoon mild ancho chili powder

continued...

SQUASH AND WOOD EAR MUSHROOMS Preheat the oven to 375°F. Have ready a large baking sheet and a sheet of aluminum foil large enough to cover the baking sheet.

In a small bowl, combine the oil with the cloves, sugar, kalonji seeds and salt. Arrange the slices of squash in a single layer on the baking sheet. Using your hands (wear rubber gloves if need be), massage all of the oil and spice mixture into the squash, making sure each piece is well coated. Be sure to include the cloves; they don't easily stick to the squash. Loosely cover the squash with the foil and bake for 25 minutes.

While the squash is baking, place the wood ear mushrooms in a medium bowl, cover them with the hot tap water (ensure they are all wet and well covered) and allow to soak for 30 minutes. Place the saffron for the curry in a medium bowl, add the ½ cup of hot water and allow to soak for 30 minutes.

SAFFRON CURRY In a medium pot, heat the ghee (or butter or oil) on medium-high heat for 1 minute. Sprinkle in the cumin seeds and allow them to sizzle for 15 to 20 seconds. Add the turmeric, cayenne and salt and stir. Cook for 30 seconds, then add the coconut milk and the ¾ cup water, stir well and bring to a boil. Reduce the heat to low and continue to cook the curry, stirring, for 5 minutes, or until little orange droplets of oil rise to the top of the pot. Stir in the saffron and its water and turn off the heat.

FINISH SQUASH AND MUSHROOMS Remove the squash from the oven, carefully lift the edge of the foil (as steam will escape) and insert the tip of a knife in the squash to be sure it is soft. If it is not, bake for another 5 minutes. Set aside the squash.

Drain the mushrooms in a fine-mesh sieve. Using scissors (or your hands), cut (or tear) the larger mushroom pieces so you have 18 more or less equally sized pieces.

TOMATO MASALA Combine the oil, tomatoes and ancho chili powder in a small pot and heat on medium-high heat, while stirring, for 3 to 5 minutes. Once the mixture is boiling, turn off the heat.

TO SERVE Place equal dollops of the tomato masala in the middle of each of 6 plates. On each plate, arrange 3 wood ear mushroom pieces around the masala. Set the squash slices on top of and around the wood ears so that the brownish-black edges are visible. Pour saffron curry over the squash.

SUGGESTED PAIRINGS
THIS IS ONE OF THE FEW INDIAN DISHES THAT STANDS ON ITS OWN.

ROASTED SPICY OKRA WITH WALNUTS AND JELLY BEANS

10 to 12 ounces chopped okra (remove the caps if you are using fresh okra)

⅓ cup + 1 tablespoon cooking oil

2 teaspoons salt

1 teaspoon ground cayenne pepper

1 cup finely chopped onions (1 medium-large)

⅓ cup chopped walnuts

4 lime leaves OR 12 to 16 fresh curry leaves

1 tablespoon ground cumin

½ tablespoon ground coriander

½ teaspoon ground star anise

½ teaspoon ground cinnamon

1 teaspoon mango powder (break up any clumps)

1 ½ to 2 teaspoons toasted or roasted sesame seeds

¼ cup jelly beans, cut in thirds

Meeru runs every morning, and one entire summer and autumn during her runs she paid close attention to all the various flowers blooming in Vancouver. She was particularly impressed with the autumn hydrangea, which maintained its beauty and dignity all the way through to its death in November. The okra in this recipe represents the flower's autumn green leaves, the sesame seeds are the browning of those leaves, and the jelly beans are sweet reminders of the summer's blue and pink petals. Jelly beans with a spicy curry are an unconventional combination, but Meeru wanted the sweetness and bright colours. At Vij's, we always use organic jelly beans (for their superior flavour) and we highly recommend them. You can find them at organic grocery stores. We serve okra on the Mildly Curried Beef Short Ribs (page 211), which represent the soil, and with white Basmati rice, which represents the light late-autumn snow. This dish also works well as a hearty and spicy topping for some of our lesser-spiced dishes. Or use it to dress up plain white rice or boiled potatoes or even a barbecued steak.

While okra is a beloved vegetable in India, many North Americans are wary of its potentially "slimy" texture. Indians often fry the okra and make sure it is cooked thoroughly to take away any sliminess yet retain its slight bitterness. Here we bake the okra instead, which uses less oil and gets rid of the sliminess but still keeps the lovely bitterness. Finding fresh okra is definitely worth the effort for its texture and taste. Be sure to rinse each okra and then wipe it with a paper towel to remove the tiny yet slightly spiky bits on it. Frozen okra is also worthy of this recipe, but take it out of its bag and thaw it beforehand. Watch your oven temperature closely when you bake the okra: you want to bake it enough to dry out the inside but avoid burning the outside. Stir it halfway through the baking to help prevent this from happening.

SERVES 4 AS A SIDE DISH OR TOPPING
PREP & COOKING TIME: 35 MINUTES

IF YOU ARE USING thawed frozen okra, spread a tea towel or a cotton cloth on a baking sheet and spread the okra on the tray in a single layer. Place another tea towel on top of the okra and press down very gently to remove any extra water.

Preheat the oven to 300°F. Arrange the okra on a large baking sheet. Sprinkle with 1 tablespoon of the oil, 1 teaspoon of the salt and ½ teaspoon of the cayenne. Rub this mixture into the okra pieces until they are well coated. Bake for 7 minutes. Stir the okra so it doesn't stick to the pan, and bake for another 6 to 8 minutes. The okra will be darker—a shade of green-brown—when it's done. Set aside.

Heat the ⅓ cup of oil in a frying pan on medium-high heat. Add the onions and sauté for 8 minutes, or until darkish brown. Stir in the walnuts and the lime (or curry) leaves and sauté for 1 minute. Add the cumin, coriander, star anise, cinnamon, and 1 teaspoon of the salt and ½ teaspoon of the cayenne. Sauté for 2 minutes more. Stir in the baked okra and turn off the heat. Stir in the mango powder.

TO SERVE Scoop the okra onto a large platter and garnish with the sesame seeds and jelly beans. Serve immediately.

SUGGESTED PAIRINGS
MILDLY CURRIED BEEF SHORT RIBS (PAGE 211)
SPICED SEMOLINA AND ALMOND MASALA ON ORANGE ROUNDS (PAGE 74)
MILD TURMERIC AND GHEE CHICKEN CURRY (PAGE 192)

CREAMY FENUGREEK AND CUMIN POTATOES

2 pounds new potatoes, unpeeled

2 ½ teaspoons salt

8 to 9 cups water

1 ½ cups full-fat sour cream

¼ to ⅓ cup cooking oil

½ tablespoon kalonji seeds

¼ cup chopped garlic (9 to 12 medium cloves)

¼ teaspoon asafoetida

2 tablespoons finely chopped ginger

1 tablespoon ground cumin

1 teaspoon turmeric

1 teaspoon ground fenugreek seeds

1 teaspoon ground cayenne pepper

½ tablespoon dried green fenugreek leaves

Marc Bricault is a good friend and the designer of our Vij's, Rangoli and My Shanti restaurants. He's also a fan of the revered spinach/mustard greens and paneer dish saag paneer, a traditional North Indian dish that Meeru isn't a fan of, even though she is a big fan of the greens and paneer—just not together. Meeru wanted to experiment with different additions to the saag that would include different textures and some bouncy flavours. This recipe is the result. We serve these potatoes either on the side or on top of Saag (page 114).

When Marc first saw this potato dish alongside the saag, in place of paneer, he was skeptical (but smiling because this wasn't the first time he was trying some unheard-of Indian combinations of Meeru's or Vikram's). But once he tasted how delicious it was, he visibly relaxed. So here's a warning to diehard traditional saag paneer fans: replacing the paneer with potatoes may be a blasphemy, but it's a beautiful one.

If you don't have hours to make the saag, you can serve these potatoes as a side dish or under most of the other main-dish curries in this book. Soaking the potatoes for a few hours in salted water makes for softer-textured and subliminally salted potatoes, especially if you keep them whole. It is not necessary, but if you have the time, we recommend it.

SERVES 6

PREP & COOKING TIME: 45 MINUTES + 3 HOURS TO SOAK THE POTATOES

WASH AND SCRUB the potatoes. In a deep, narrow pot, combine 1 ½ teaspoons of the salt and 5 to 6 cups of the water and stir to dissolve the salt. Add the potatoes, ensuring they are submerged, and allow to soak for 3 hours.

In a medium bowl, whisk together the sour cream and 3 cups of the water. Set aside.

Heat the oil in a medium-large pot on medium-high heat for 1 minute. Sprinkle in the kalonji seeds and allow them to sizzle for 30 to 45 seconds. Stir in the garlic and sauté for 2 minutes, or until light golden. Sprinkle in the asafoetida and sauté for

30 seconds, then stir in the ginger. Add the cumin, turmeric, fenugreek seeds, cayenne and 1 teaspoon of the salt; sauté for 2 minutes, or until the oil glistens on the spices. Gently pour in the sour cream mixture and stir well.

Drain the potatoes. If they're on the larger size, cut them in half. Add them to the sour cream curry and bring to a boil. Reduce the heat to a simmer and cook, covered, for 20 to 25 minutes. Poke the potatoes with a sharp knife to be sure they are cooked through. Stir in the fenugreek leaves and cook, uncovered, for 3 to 4 minutes more.

TO SERVE Serve these potatoes under your main dish, as you would serve rice.

SUGGESTED PAIRINGS
SAAG (PAGE 114)
SPROUTED LENTIL, BELL PEPPER AND CARROT SALAD (PAGE 129)
DUCK BREAST AND FRESH MANGOES (PAGE 201)

COCONUT JAPANESE-INDIAN GREEN BEAN CURRY

½ cup cooking oil

1 medium red onion, finely chopped

½ cup chopped green onions, white and green parts

¾ cup unsweetened dried coconut flakes

1 ½ cups finely chopped fresh tomatoes (6 medium)

1 tablespoon ground coriander

½ tablespoon turmeric

1 teaspoon crushed cayenne pepper

2 pounds green beans, trimmed and chopped into ½-inch pieces

2 tablespoons ketchup

½ to 1 ½ cups water

2 teaspoons Worcestershire sauce

⅓ to ½ cup chopped cilantro, including stems

1 tablespoon soy sauce

salt to taste

In 2010, during the Vancouver Winter Olympics, Meeru hosted a lunch at Rangoli for a group of Japanese media people. Vikram served the food while Meeru joined our guests at the table. We served them half-sized portions of a large variety of our curries from both the Vij's and Rangoli menus. At the end of the meal, Meeru asked the photographer in the group two questions: (1) Why does the Japanese government support whale hunting? and (2) What is the most popular dish in Japan? His answer to the first question was that it's difficult for outsiders to understand. (He's right; we don't.) To the second question, he answered Japanese curry.

This was a revelation to our entire family, considering how much we love Japanese food and all of Hayao Miyazaki's anime films—all four of us in equal measure. Miyazaki films belong to the slim category of movies that celebrate the joys of being brave girls who don't understand why anyone would think they were any less capable than boys. This has been one of the most important messages we wish to instill in our daughters and, in fact, all of our staff. To hear the word "curry" added to "Japanese" was like feeling snow on our faces for the first time.

On Meeru's next trip to Singapore to visit Vikram's sister and her family, she booked an eight-hour layover at Narita Airport in Tokyo. With Nanaki and Shanik in tow, Meeru ordered one bowl of every "curry" on the menu at Narita Airport's restaurants (realizing that this was airport cuisine). There are two things the three of us will always remember about this day: the thrill the girls experienced being able to eat so many "thick white noodles" (udon) without Meeru worrying about them becoming constipated, and Shanik's nonstop insistence that Meeru buy her the Totoro Catbus stuffed animal that cost the equivalent of more than a hundred Canadian dollars. (Totoro Catbus is one of Shanik's favourite Miyazaki characters from childhood. And though Meeru refused, Shanik's aunt gave her the money to buy the Catbus during their return layover.) Though the Japanese curries were a bit off the Indian curry mark for Meeru and Nanaki, their sweet flavour and thick texture were a hit with Shanik. It was after this trip that Shanik started cooking Japanese food at home. And the Narita curries were good enough to lead us to cook Indo-Japanese.

This is the first recipe inspired by our Narita trip, and it's incredibly versatile. Shanik enjoys this dish as a complement to her homemade cucumber and avocado rolls. (Nanaki and Shanik, much to the bewilderment of their father, prefer to eat Indian curries on sushi rice instead of Basmati.) It can also be served as a soup to go with sushi or Basmati rice or, if you make it drier, as a side dish to accompany just about anything, including a grilled steak. To make a dinner entrée, just double all the ingredients in this recipe—except the green beans. Add 2 pounds of raw tofu or chicken or potatoes. The key is to keep the ratios roughly the same—too much Worcestershire sauce or ketchup can cover up the Indian spices. Be sure to add any extra or substitute ingredients according to their cooking time.

SERVES 8
PREP & COOKING TIME: 45 MINUTES

IN A LARGE frying pan or a wok, heat the oil on medium heat. Add the red onions and sauté for 5 minutes, or until they sweat but before they begin to turn golden at the edges. Stir in the green onions and sauté for 1 minute. Add the coconut flakes, stir well and sauté for 2 minutes. Stir in the tomatoes and immediately add the coriander, turmeric and cayenne. Cook the masala for 4 to 5 minutes, or until the oil glistens on the tomatoes.

Stir in the green beans and cook for 3 minutes, stirring regularly. Add the ketchup and anywhere from ½ cup (for a drier style) to 1 ½ cups water, stir well and continue cooking until the liquid is boiling and the green beans are cooked through, about 5 minutes. Stir in the Worcestershire sauce and cilantro. Turn off the heat and stir in the soy sauce. Season with salt, if necessary.

TO SERVE Transfer the curry to a large bowl and serve family style.

SUGGESTED PAIRINGS
CLAY POT SAFFRON CHICKEN AND RICE (PAGE 198)
CARROT AND SEMOLINA CREPES (PAGE 146)
LENTIL CURRY WITH SAUTÉED EGGPLANT, POTATOES AND FENNEL (PAGE 156)

ASSORTED MUSHROOMS AND WINTER SQUASH CURRY

1 ounce dried porcini mushrooms

1 cup very hot tap water

¼ cup cooking oil

½ cup puréed fresh or canned tomatoes

1 tablespoon ground cumin

2 teaspoons salt

1 teaspoon turmeric

1 teaspoon ground cayenne pepper

3 pounds kabocha, acorn or butternut squash, seeded, peeled if you like, and cut into 2-inch cubes

8 ounces portobello OR 5 ounces shiitake mushrooms

1 cup whipping cream

½ tablespoon dried green fenugreek leaves

1 juicy lemon, cut into 8 wedges

This curry is particularly good in the fall, when mushrooms are at their prime and squash are ready for harvest. It's an easy curry to make, as the bulk of the work is cutting up the squash. Use a large, sharp, sturdy knife and a cutting board. If your knife isn't sharp enough to cut smaller pieces, leave them larger and cook them for an additional 10 to 15 minutes. Nanaki and Shanik prefer the soft texture of this dish that we get from peeling the squash completely, but at Vij's we partially peel them because we like the colour contrast and because the peel helps the squash to keep its texture when it is reheated. Try it both ways and see which you like better.

Sometimes we make this recipe with shiitake mushrooms, sometimes with portobellos. Use whichever one you prefer. We leave the shiitakes whole but cut the portobellos into slices. Since you are not using any onion or garlic in this curry, make sure your cumin and dried fenugreek are fresh and have a strong aroma. We enjoy a squirt of lemon to finish the curry, but serve the lemon wedges on the side so that diners can decide for themselves how much or little they want. We find that this dish tastes best served over plain quinoa (prepared with just a little salt) or with an Indian flatbread. Or we make the Quinoa and Cauliflower Salad (page 130) but omit the turmeric.

SERVES 8

PREP & COOKING TIME: 1 ¼ HOURS

(INCLUDING THE 30 MINUTES SOAKING TIME)

PLACE THE DRIED porcini mushrooms in a small bowl, add the hot water and allow to soak for 30 minutes. Set a fine-mesh sieve over a small bowl. Strain the mushrooms through the sieve, reserving the mushrooms and the soaking water separately. Set aside.

Preheat the oven to 375°F. Heat the oil in a small pan on medium-high heat and add the tomatoes, cumin, salt, turmeric and cayenne. Stir, cook for 2 minutes, then immediately remove from the heat.

In a casserole dish with a tight lid, combine the squash, porto-bello mushrooms (do not add the shiitakes at this time) and spiced tomatoes; mix well. Add the porcini water and the whipping cream, stirring gently until well combined. Using a sharp knife, roughly chop the soaked porcini mushrooms and add them to the casserole dish. Cover and bake for 40 minutes. Poke a piece of the squash with a small knife to see if it is soft and cooked through. If not, return to the oven for 5 minutes more.

Once the squash is cooked, carefully stir in the fenugreek leaves and shiitake mushrooms (if you are using them). The curry will be very hot. Return the casserole dish to the oven and bake for 5 minutes.

TO SERVE Bring the casserole dish to the table and serve family style—warn diners that the dish is hot! Or serve in individual bowls. Serve with the lemon wedges on the side.

SUGGESTED PAIRINGS
QUINOA AND CAULIFLOWER SALAD (PAGE 130)
NAVY BEANS IN EGG AND TOMATO MASALA (PAGE 158)
BROWN RICE AND YELLOW CHANNA DAAL PILAF (PAGE 138)

YAMS, MUSHROOMS, GREEN BEANS AND ASPARAGUS IN CUMIN AND FENUGREEK CURRY

⅓ cup + 1 tablespoon cooking oil

2 teaspoons Garam Masala (page 23)

2 ½ teaspoons salt

8 to 10 ounces mushrooms, whole or sliced (see note at right)

1 tablespoon cumin seeds

1 cup finely chopped onions (1 medium-large)

1 tablespoon finely chopped garlic (3 to 4 medium cloves)

1 tablespoon chopped ginger

1 teaspoon turmeric

1 teaspoon crushed cayenne pepper

1 ½ pounds yams, peeled and cut into 1 ½-inch pieces

4 cups water

2 tablespoons chickpea flour

10 ounces green beans, chopped into ¼-inch pieces

2 cups whipping cream

½ tablespoon dried green fenugreek leaves

8 ounces asparagus tips OR broccoli florets

SUGGESTED PAIRINGS
CAULIFLOWER AND POTATO IN TOMATO MASALA (PAGE 111)
SPICY RICE PILAF FOR LOCAL VEGETABLES (PAGE 136)
SWEET AND SAVOURY MILLET PILAF WITH FENNEL SEEDS (PAGE 143)

The combination of dried green fenugreek leaves and cream may sound like a culinary cliché in the Vij's world, but it leads to an endless number of wonderful pairings. In this curry, this combination brings out the subtle nutty flavour of the chickpea flour with the earthy mushrooms and sweet yams. Although the yams and mushrooms are key components of this recipe, you can use whichever other vegetables you prefer.

We use an assortment of mushrooms when we make this dish, either slicing them thinly if they are "meatier" mushrooms such as portobellos or using them whole if they are lighter mushrooms such as enoki or shiitakes. Mushrooms are a powerhouse of nutrients, especially B vitamins, minerals, enzymes and antioxidants. However, they fully absorb whatever they are growing in, so it's important to know where your mushrooms came from or to buy organic. Serve this curry with plain rice, bread, naan or chapatti.

SERVES 6 TO 8
PREP & COOKING TIME: 45 MINUTES TO 1 HOUR

IN A VERY SMALL pot, heat the 1 tablespoon of oil on medium-high heat for 1 minute. Stir in the garam masala and immediately turn off the heat. Stir in ½ teaspoon of the salt. Empty all the oil and garam masala into a medium bowl, add the mushrooms and mix well. Set aside.

Heat the ⅓ cup of oil in a large, heavy-bottomed pot on medium-high heat for 1 minute. Sprinkle in the cumin and allow the seeds to sizzle for 15 to 20 seconds. Add the onions and sauté until dark brown, 10 to 12 minutes. Stir in the garlic and sauté for 1 minute, and then stir in the ginger. Add the turmeric, cayenne and 2 teaspoons of the salt and sauté for 1 minute. Add the yams and cook, stirring, for 3 minutes. (This step will coat the yams in oil and prevent them from becoming too mushy in the curry.)

Pour the water into a medium bowl, add the chickpea flour and whisk well. Add this mixture to the pot and bring to a boil. Reduce the heat to medium, cover and cook for 10 minutes. Poke a small sharp knife into a piece of yam to see if it is nearly soft. (You want the yams to be slightly undercooked at this point.) If not, continue to cook, checking regularly, for another 5 to 10 minutes. Add the green beans.

Place the whipping cream in a small bowl. Stir in about ½ cup of the hot curry to temper it, then add this cream to the pot of hot curry. Stir in the fenugreek leaves and bring to a boil. Add the asparagus tips (or broccoli florets) and stir. Turn off the heat. The asparagus (or broccoli) will cook in the heat of the curry.

If you are ready to serve the curry, stir in the mushrooms. Otherwise, stir in the mushrooms after you reheat the curry for serving.

TO SERVE Divide the curry among individual bowls and serve.

CREAMY YAM CURRY

1 or 2 pounds yams, unpeeled

¼ cup cooking oil

3 tablespoons chopped ginger

1 tablespoon ground yellow mustard seeds

1 teaspoon ground fenugreek seeds

1 tablespoon mild ancho chili powder

½ tablespoon salt

1 teaspoon turmeric

1 teaspoon ground cayenne pepper

2 cups vegetable, meat or chicken stock

¼ cup lemon juice

6 cups whipping cream

Neither Vikram nor Meeru grew up eating yams at home. In India, these vegetables are served as street food, slow-cooked over a charcoal barbecue at the side of the road and eaten piping hot with salt and black pepper. When he didn't have access to the fried or spicy street foods he preferred, Vikram would occasionally enjoy one of these yams. Meeru had her first taste of yam as part of a Thanksgiving school lunch in elementary school. Although she generally liked these lunches because they didn't contain any ginger or turmeric like her meals at home, she wasn't impressed with the yam's mushy sweetness. Boiled yams were popular as baby food, though, so it wasn't until Nanaki was born that either of us actually bought and cooked one. As Vikram has always been a stickler about not wasting food, he would gobble up any chunks of yam that Nanaki left uneaten. Adding salt, black pepper and some mango pickle to these leftover chunks made them delicious. We decided that with the right spices and ingredients, yam could be a special addition to Indian curries.

This rich, creamy curry can be eaten alone as a soup with salad or used to top a non-Indian steak or roast chicken. For a soup, use the higher amount of yams and include the stock. If you make this curry as a topping, use the lesser amount of yams and leave out the stock. You won't need to adjust the spices at all.

SERVES 6

PREP & COOKING TIME: 50 MINUTES (INCLUDING TIME FOR THE YAMS TO COOL)

CUT THE YAMS in half and place them in a medium pot of water. Cover and bring to a boil on high heat. Reduce the heat to medium and boil for 25 minutes, or until the yams are soft when poked with a knife. Drain the yams, allow them to cool enough that you can handle them, and then peel and chop them roughly (all the pieces should be bite-sized). Depending on how soft they are, you can even break the yams into chunks with your hands. Set aside.

While the yams are boiling, make the curry. Place the oil and ginger in a medium pot on medium heat and cook for 2 to 3 minutes, or until the ginger is sizzling. Add the mustard seeds, fenugreek, ancho chili powder, salt, turmeric and cayenne. Stir and sauté for 2 minutes. Turn off the heat. Stir in the stock (if using) and the lemon juice, then stir in the whipping cream.

Return the curry to medium-low heat and, while stirring occasionally, bring to a gentle simmer (if you boil it too quickly, the cream may split). Cover and cook for 5 minutes, or until tiny beads of oil glisten on top. Stir in the yams and mix well. Turn off the heat.

When you are ready to serve, heat the curry on medium heat just until it reaches a boil.

TO SERVE Serve this curry like a soup in individual bowls. If you prefer, pour it into a serving bowl and ladle it over individual meals as a gravy-like topping.

SUGGESTED PAIRINGS
INDIAN-JAPANESE CHICKEN-VEGETABLE
SOBA NOODLE CURRY (PAGE 196)
SEARED TILAPIA WITH DRIED FRUIT SPRINKLE (PAGE 176)
CHICKPEA AND SPROUTED LENTIL CAKES (PAGE 152)

ZUCCHINI, SQUASH AND POTATO SAUTÉ

3 pounds total of zucchini, yellow squash and/or Yukon Gold or new potatoes, unpeeled

¼ to ⅓ cup coconut oil

½ tablespoon black mustard seeds

10 to 12 fresh curry leaves (optional)

1 teaspoon ground coriander

1 teaspoon turmeric

½ tablespoon salt

½ teaspoon ground black pepper

1 ½ cups chopped fresh spinach (optional)

One evening when Meeru and Vikram were both working, each thought the other had made dinner for the girls. Nanaki was fifteen at the time and she made some plain long-grain rice, which she topped with a bit of crumbled toasted nori (the dried seaweed used to make sushi rolls). In the fridge she found leftovers of this sauté, which she reheated and poured over the rice. She added some soy sauce, and it was apparently "the best dinner ever—and Mom should sell it at Rangoli." Sure enough, now we always have some version of this easy and mild-tasting vegetable dish on our menus—minus the nori and soy sauce!

The uses of this dish are limited only by your imagination. Mix and match as much or as little of each vegetable as you wish.

SERVES 6

PREP & COOKING TIME: 30 MINUTES

CUT ALL the vegetables in rounds of the same thickness. If you're using Yukon Gold potatoes, first cut them in half lengthwise and then slice them (you'll have half-moon pieces). Place the potatoes in a bowl and set aside the other vegetables.

Heat the coconut oil in a medium frying pan on high heat for 45 seconds to 1 minute. Sprinkle in the mustard seeds and allow them to sizzle until you hear the very first pops, 30 to 45 seconds. Turn off the heat. Keeping your face away from the pot, add the curry leaves (they may splatter with the heat). They will shrivel up. Add the coriander, turmeric, salt and black pepper; stir gently. If the spices are sizzling, add the potatoes. If they are not, turn on the heat to medium and cook the spices for 2 minutes. Add the potatoes and sauté for 5 to 10 minutes, or until soft and cooked through. Once the potatoes are cooked, add the zucchini and squash and sauté for 3 to 4 minutes. Stir in the spinach and remove from the heat.

TO SERVE Scoop the vegetables into a large serving bowl and serve family style. Serve immediately.

SUGGESTED PAIRINGS

SAVOURY INDIAN TRUFFLES (PAGE 62)

SIMPLE GRILLED CHICKEN WITH OPTIONAL SPICE SPRINKLE (PAGE 190)

COCONUT PRAWN CURRY (PAGE 168)

GRILLED SQUASH WITH SUGAR-ROASTED BEETS AND CUMIN-SPICED ONIONS

SUGAR-ROASTED BEETS

1 ½ pounds beets, peeled and chopped into 1 ½-inch pieces

1 tablespoon + 1 teaspoon ghee, melted

2 tablespoons raw or demerara sugar

1 teaspoon salt

½ teaspoon ground cayenne pepper

½ teaspoon turmeric

2 cups water

We have had this deceptively simple-tasting dish on our Vij's menu for a long time because we insist that our heavy-meat-eating customers order it along with their mains. It's a very healthy dish whose layers of squash, beets and onions are the perfect balance of mild Indian flavours with a nice cayenne zing. It makes a great companion to any meat dishes, not just Indian ones.

This dish takes time and effort, so we make it at home only for special dinner parties. If you make it more than once, it will most likely be faster and easier the second time. If you're not ready to invest that much time, make just one "layer," or part of the dish, and add it to another meal. For example, the sugar-roasted beets are a great, simple side for most curries that are not already sweet. Or prepare just the grilled squash topped with the onions as a side dish for your meal.

We like acorn or butternut squash for this recipe, but you can use any orange-fleshed squash—there are so many to choose from in the Pacific Northwest. Winter squash keep for a relatively long time, so they are a good vegetable to buy and you won't have to worry about them rotting in your fridge before you ever get the chance to cook with them. You can even prepare just the squash portion of this recipe and serve it as a stand-alone snack or side dish to another entrée. It is important that you use ghee (or coconut oil, if you are vegan) instead of butter because with so few spices, the caramelized flavour of ghee is a necessary addition. Start the squash while the beets are in the oven.

SERVES 6

PREP & COOKING TIME: 1 ½ TO 2 HOURS

SUGAR-ROASTED BEETS Preheat the oven to 400°F. Combine the beets, ghee, sugar, salt, cayenne and turmeric in a baking dish and mix until well combined. Pour in the water, cover and bake for 1 hour. Carefully uncover the dish and gently poke a knife through a beet to check if it's cooked through. The beets should be firm but easy to poke. If they are not yet ready, cover them and bake them for another 10 to 15 minutes. Remove from the oven and set aside in their cooking liquid.

continued...

GRILLED SQUASH

1 ½ pounds winter squash, halved, seeded and cut into ⅛-inch slices

¼ cup cooking oil

1 teaspoon mild ancho chili powder OR paprika

½ teaspoon ground cayenne pepper

½ teaspoon salt

CUMIN-SPICED ONIONS

½ cup cooking oil

1 teaspoon cumin seeds

½ teaspoon ajwain seeds

1 teaspoon crushed cayenne pepper

1 pound onions (1 large), halved lengthwise and thinly sliced

GRILLED SQUASH While the beets are roasting, in a large bowl, combine the squash, oil, ancho chili powder (or paprika), cayenne and salt; mix thoroughly. Cover and allow to stand for 30 minutes.

CUMIN-SPICED ONIONS Place a medium sieve (at least 5 inches wide) over a bowl. Heat the oil in a large frying pan on high heat for 1 minute. Add the cumin and ajwain seeds and allow them to sizzle for 20 seconds. Immediately add the cayenne and onions and sauté, stirring regularly, for 5 to 8 minutes, or until dark brown but not burned. Strain the onions through the sieve, reserving the cooking oil for another use or discarding it.

FINISH SQUASH Just before you are ready to serve, heat a stovetop grill on high. Mix the squash well in the oil and spices and then place the slices directly on the grill (set the pieces as close together as you can get them). Cook on one side for 3 minutes, until the squash goes from shiny to matte. Turn the squash over and grill it for 2 minutes.

TO SERVE Arrange the grilled squash in a large shallow serving dish. Place the sugar-roasted beets on top and pour the beet liquid over the entire dish, so the squash is sitting in the liquid. Top with the cumin-spiced onions. Serve immediately.

SUGGESTED PAIRINGS
BEEF SHORT RIBS IN KALONJI AND CREAM CURRY (PAGE 208)
LAMB POPSICLES WITH GARLIC AND RICOTTA-
FENUGREEK TOPPING (PAGE 218)
YELLOW LENTIL CURRY WITH BLACK LENTIL MASALA (PAGE 149)

CAULIFLOWER AND POTATO IN TOMATO MASALA

Throughout her life, Meeru's mother has used buying and cooking food to celebrate her milestones, mourn many losses and cope with her loneliness and isolation. As a new immigrant to the United States in the early 1970s, she discovered farmers' markets and spent hours every week selecting produce and cooking for our family and friends. Just being at the farmers' markets among other shoppers was a social outing, and she felt a kinship with them—she assumed they were all as interested in food and cooking as she was.

Whenever she has received news of the death of a relative or friend in India, she has gone into the kitchen and prepared the chai and hot snacks that Indian custom dictates a family should have ready when friends and acquaintances come to offer their condolences. For a week, the house will smell of deep-fried oil and spices. Now, after her third stroke, Meeru's mother can no longer speak or hear, and her eyes and body are weak. But she continues to cook—more and more, in fact—though her style has changed and she no longer makes the same recipes.

Just about every evening after work, Meeru's father takes his wife grocery shopping, and then she cooks all the next day. Omi is preparing more dishes than ever before, but no dish requires much standing and chopping. She purées garlic in her blender and keeps big batches of it in the fridge. She has stopped using as many onions. Instead of sautéing some onions or garlic and then mixing in her tomatoes and ginger for a "wet" masala, she has begun to cook with even more turmeric and ginger, and to add asafoetida to her dishes. (Turmeric is believed to prevent dementia and depression, and Omi seems to be using her spices to keep her brain as healthy as possible.) The kitchen exhaust cannot keep up with her Indian spices, and the Dhalwala home, clothes and bath towels smell strongly of cumin and coriander, which Omi grinds as she cooks. With this daily feast of new foods, she now feeds just about everyone in the neighbourhood and in her husband's office. And when Vikram visited Omi during a break from shooting *Dragon's Den*, she got up early on the day he was leaving so she could pack his carry-on with several kinds of Indian *paranthas* (stuffed and fried flatbreads) and her own home-made pickle. We joke that she has reached a state of Zen cooking.

⅓ cup cooking oil

1 tablespoon cumin seeds

¼ teaspoon asafoetida (optional)

2 cups chopped fresh, juicy tomatoes (5 to 6 medium)

2 tablespoons chopped garlic (6 to 7 medium cloves)

1 tablespoon thinly sliced ginger

1 tablespoon ground coriander

½ tablespoon salt

1 teaspoon turmeric

1 teaspoon ground cayenne pepper

1 pound new or Yukon Gold potatoes, cut into large slices

1 medium to large head cauliflower, cut into thick florets

½ to ¾ cup chopped fresh cilantro

continued...

One evening on a visit to Virginia, Meeru watched her mother make this "Zen stroke" cauliflower and potato curry very quickly. Since they couldn't talk about the recipe, this simple but delicious version is based on what Meeru observed and what she tasted in the final dish. The key is to use very good, "moist" ginger and garlic and both coriander and cilantro. Both the dried coriander and fresh cilantro should be very aromatic, so use only the freshest you can buy (a finely ground store-bought coriander that's been sitting in your cupboard for three months will not give you any oomph). If you are using very fresh, very finely ground coriander, you may need to use a little less.

The size you cut your cauliflower and potatoes does not matter, but try to make all the pieces about the same size. Depending on their thickness, potatoes take longer to cook, so add them to the pot first, because if you keep the cauliflower covered for too long, it will release lots of water, just like overcooked mushrooms. Serve this curry with piping-hot whole-wheat chapatti or another flatbread, breaking off bits of bread to scoop this masala directly into your mouth.

SERVES 6 TO 8

PREP & COOKING TIME: 30 MINUTES

IN A LARGE pot, combine the oil and cumin seeds. Heat on medium-high heat until the cumin sizzles for 20 seconds. Immediately add the asafoetida and allow both to sizzle for 10 seconds. Stir in the tomatoes, garlic and ginger. Reduce the heat to medium, cover and cook for 4 minutes. Stir to make sure there is still enough liquid from the tomatoes and they are not burning. Cover and cook for another 3 to 4 minutes.

Remove the lid, stir, and add the coriander, salt, turmeric and cayenne; sauté for 2 minutes. Stir in the potatoes. Reduce the heat slightly, cover and cook for 10 minutes, or until three-quarters cooked. Add the cauliflower. Stir well, increase the heat to medium-high and cook, uncovered, for 5 minutes. Reduce the heat to medium-low, cover and cook for 5 to 8 minutes, or just until both vegetables are cooked. Turn off the heat and stir in the fresh cilantro.

TO SERVE Ladle the cauliflower and potatoes into a large serving bowl or heap spoonfuls onto individual plates.

SUGGESTED PAIRINGS

BROWN BASMATI RICE, PINTO BEAN AND
VEGETABLE "CAMPER'S CURRY" (PAGE 159)

RAINBOW TROUT IN COCONUT CURRY WITH CURRY LEAVES (PAGE 179)

SAAG, TOPPED WITH THE CAULIFLOWER
AND POTATOES (PAGE 114)

SAAG (PURÉED SPINACH AND MUSTARD GREENS)

1 pound mustard greens, rapini and/or dandelion greens

1 pound spinach, stems included, washed and roughly chopped

1 pound broccoli, florets only

1 pound chopped cabbage

10 cups water

1 tablespoon salt

⅔ cup corn flour

½ cup ghee

1 ½ cups very finely chopped onions (1 large)

3 tablespoons chopped garlic (9 to 10 medium cloves)

3 tablespoons chopped ginger

2 tablespoons chopped jalapeño pepper (1 large)

7 to 9 ounces Paneer (page 38), cut into 1-inch cubes (optional)

Saag is often combined with Paneer (page 38) to make saag paneer, which we call northern India's queen bee of traditional vegetarian dishes. There is no single recipe for saag. Both Vikram's and Meeru's mothers regularly made saag paneer when we were growing up, and all our Punjabi kitchen staff have their own family versions of it. We serve it in all our restaurants, but it is slightly different in each one because our cooks adapt the recipe to their style of making it. Saag paneer is usually served with corn flour chapattis. Vikram loves this dish, whereas Meeru finds it too mushy. Meeru also dislikes the corn flour chapattis. Her compromise is to make the saag but serve it in "blasphemous ways" (see suggested pairings below) that give it more texture.

Making saag is a labour of love, but it's not difficult to learn. To be an excellent maker of saag, you need to make it regularly and to feel comfortable with your preferred combination of greens. In a nutshell, you want a ratio of 1 pound bitter greens to 3 pounds mellow greens. If you're not fond of rapini, substitute mustard greens, collards, turnip, dandelion or mizuna greens. Or just use 3 pounds of spinach and forgo the broccoli florets and cabbage.

For a basic saag, follow this recipe (without adding the paneer) and serve it with regular chapattis, corn flour chapattis, naan or baguette. Or make the traditional saag paneer by stirring cubes of paneer into the cooked and puréed greens.

SERVES 10

PREP & COOKING TIME: 2 ½ HOURS

(INCLUDING TIME TO MAKE THE PANEER)

IN A LARGE pot, combine the rapini and/or greens, spinach, broccoli, cabbage, water and salt. Bring to a boil on high heat, partially cover, reduce the heat to low and simmer for 2 hours, stirring every 20 minutes or so. Remove from the heat. Sprinkle in the corn flour, making sure to distribute it throughout the pot so that it does not clump. With an electric beater or an immersion blender, purée the greens and corn flour mixture until smooth and thoroughly combined. Return the pot to medium heat and cook the greens, covered, for 10 minutes to cook the corn flour.

Melt the ghee in a frying pan on high heat. Add the onions and sauté for 6 to 8 minutes, or until medium brown. Stir in the garlic and sauté for another 2 to 3 minutes, or until the garlic is golden and the onions are a darker brown. Stir in the ginger and jalapeños and sauté for 1 minute. Stir this mixture into the cooked greens. Gently stir to combine. Fold in the paneer.

TO SERVE Pour the saag into a large serving bowl and serve piping hot. Be sure to provide smaller dinner bowls for each person, as saag paneer is a bit runny and has such a distinct flavour that we don't usually put it on the same plate as our bread and other curries.

SUGGESTED PAIRINGS
GRILLED SQUASH WITH SUGAR-ROASTED BEETS AND
CUMIN-SPICED ONIONS (PAGE 108)
CREAMY FENUGREEK AND CUMIN POTATOES (PAGE 96)
CAULIFLOWER AND POTATO IN
TOMATO MASALA (PAGE 111)

BITTER GOURD WITH POTATOES AND ONIONS

10 to 12 ounces bitter gourd (about 5), cut into thin rounds

1 teaspoon salt

1 teaspoon lemon juice

½ cup cooking oil

1 tablespoon + 1 teaspoon cumin seeds

1 medium onion, quartered and thinly sliced

½ cup chickpea flour

1 tablespoon chopped ginger

1 tablespoon ground coriander

½ tablespoon turmeric

1 teaspoon ground cayenne pepper

1 pound Yukon Gold potatoes, chopped into ¼-inch pieces

¾ cup water

½ pound finely chopped green bell peppers

Most North Americans aren't familiar with bitter gourd. Indians either love it or hate it, but they all respect this vegetable for its health value. There are bitter gourd pills and juices that are said to help purify the blood and help reduce blood sugar levels in diabetics. You will find this vegetable in most Asian grocery stores, but they may sell both Chinese and Indian bitter gourds (also sold as bitter melon). The two look and taste different, and for this recipe you want Indian bitter gourd. Its bitterness is immediate and strong rather than slowly creeping up on you, as the flavour of Chinese bitter gourd does. Don't worry about the size, but do choose firm vegetables with just a bit of softness. If your gourd is hard and fat and looks like it might pop, put it back on the shelf.

We marinate the bitter gourd in a little salt and lemon juice to take the sting out of the bitterness before using this vegetable in our recipes. Once prepared, bitter gourd is salty like anchovies or olives. At Vij's, we serve this recipe with Duck Breast and Fresh Mangoes (page 201), but you can serve it with any type of flatbread and a lentil or vegetable curry. Yogurt (page 34) or Raita (page 33) also tastes delicious on the side.

SERVES 5 TO 6
PREP & COOKING TIME: 1 ½ HOURS

COMBINE the bitter gourd rounds, salt and lemon in a medium bowl, mix well and set aside for 1 hour. After you mix the lemon and salt thoroughly the first time, do not mix it again—allow any liquid to remain at the bottom of the bowl as the bitter gourd drains. Remove the gourds, discard the liquid and return the vegetables to the bowl.

Heat the oil in a large frying pan on medium-high heat for 1 minute. Add the cumin seeds and allow them to sizzle for 15 seconds. Add the onions, and stir once to spread them evenly across the pan. Cook, without stirring, for 4 to 6 minutes, or until the edges of the onions become nicely browned. Reduce the heat to medium, add the chickpea flour and stir well. Cook, stirring regularly, for 4 minutes, or until the flour turns a darker shade of

SUGGESTED PAIRINGS
GREENS SAUTÉED IN BROWN SUGAR AND TURMERIC WITH CHICKPEAS IN TAMARIND CURRY (PAGE 154)
MILDLY CURRIED BEEF SHORT RIBS (PAGE 211)
CREAMY YAM CURRY (PAGE 104)

golden brown. Add the ginger, coriander, turmeric and cayenne; sauté for 3 to 4 minutes. Stir in the potatoes and water and cook, uncovered and stirring regularly, for 5 minutes. Add the bitter gourd rounds and stir well. Cook, stirring regularly, for 10 minutes. Stir in the bell peppers and cook for another few minutes, until the peppers soften but are still slightly crunchy.

TO SERVE Spoon portions of this drier-style curry onto individual plates. We eat this dish with our hands, using bite-sized pieces of flatbread to scoop the vegetables into our mouth.

NORTH INDIAN STUFFED SPICY BITTER GOURD

12 Indian bitter gourds, about 2 ounces each

1 tablespoon + ½ teaspoon salt

⅓ cup cooking oil + more for deep-frying

1 large onion, quartered and thinly sliced (2 cups)

1 tablespoon chopped ginger

1 tablespoon ground cumin

1 tablespoon ground coriander

1 tablespoon mild ancho chili powder

1 teaspoon ground cayenne pepper

¼ teaspoon ground cloves OR cinnamon (optional)

1 medium potato, boiled, peeled and mashed

½ tablespoon mango powder (break up any clumps)

Stuffed spicy bitter gourds are to northern Indians (who love this vegetable) as homemade apple pie is to North Americans: it's a dish that sums up comfort, tradition and culture. This northern Indian way to prepare bitter gourds takes time, but it's a delicacy that has no flavour comparison in any other culture. If you make this dish for Indian friends, they will love your effort and you will earn their respect forever, irrespective of how the food tastes! We strongly recommend that you set aside a day for cooking this recipe and serve the stuffed bitter gourds the traditional way—with a lentil curry, an Indian salad and/or Raita (page 33), with rice and/or naan or chapattis on the side.

Both Vikram's and Meeru's mothers prepare a version that's close to this recipe. (Meeru's mom uses more spices.) This is one of Meeru's favourite dishes, and her father complains that the only time he gets to eat it is when Meeru visits. The potatoes in this recipe are not traditional but they soften the flavours just slightly and make it easier to stuff and fry the gourds without all the spices falling out.

You will need to open your kitchen windows or have a strong exhaust fan going when making this dish. Otherwise, your home will smell for a few days of sautéed onions, strong spices and frying oil. If you do make this dish, we'd love to hear from you.

SERVES 6 (2 STUFFED BITTER GOURDS PER PERSON)
PREP & COOKING TIME: 6 HOURS (INCLUDING SOAKING TIME)

SUGGESTED PAIRINGS
YELLOW LENTIL CURRY WITH BLACK LENTIL MASALA (PAGE 149)
LENTIL CURRY WITH SAUTÉED EGGPLANT, POTATOES AND FENNEL (PAGE 156)
NAPA CABBAGE IN TOMATO MASALA SALAD (PAGE 59)

USING THE SIDE of a spoon (not a peeler, which removes too much skin), scrape the outer skin from the bitter gourds. Discard the skin. Using a paring knife, cut a slit in the flesh of each gourd from one end to the other deep enough to reach in with your fingers and take out all the seeds, leaving the gourds hollow. Discard the seeds. Using your hands, thoroughly rub the gourds with 1 tablespoon of the salt. Set the gourds in a large bowl and allow them to sit for 4 hours.

continued...

Before you make the filling, turn on your exhaust fan. In a frying pan, heat the ⅓ cup of oil on medium heat. Add the onions and sauté for 8 minutes, or until a darker golden. Stir in the ginger. Add the cumin, coriander, ancho chili powder, cayenne, cloves or cinnamon (if using) and the ½ teaspoon of salt. Stir and sauté for 2 to 3 minutes, until this masala is shiny and the oil glistens on top. Set aside 1 teaspoon of the mashed potato. Mix the rest of the potatoes and the mango powder into the masala. Remove the filling from the heat and set aside.

Using a tea towel, dry each bitter gourd individually, gently squeezing any excess water out into the towel. (Do not feel tempted to rinse the gourds to remove the salt.) Line a baking sheet or large plate with paper towels and set it next to the stove.

Heat 2 inches of oil in a wide, deep, heavy-bottomed pan on medium-high heat for 5 minutes. To check if the oil is hot enough, drop a ½-teaspoon ball of the mashed potato into the oil. If it rises immediately and starts to sizzle, the oil is hot enough. If a lot of smoke is coming from the oil, it is too hot—reduce your heat to medium. Once the oil is hot enough, carefully lower the bitter gourds into the oil and fry them for 5 minutes, or until uniformly golden. Stir them regularly with a slotted spoon. Remove the bitter gourds as they are cooked and place them on the paper towel–lined baking sheet. Allow them to cool for 20 minutes.

To stuff the gourds, divide the potato-onion filling into 12 portions. Use a teaspoon and your hands to push the filling in through each slit, distributing it evenly along the length of the gourd. Close the bitter gourds as much as you can so that the masala won't spill out when you reheat them. If they are warm, go ahead and serve them as is. However, if they have cooled and you want to serve them hot, arrange them tightly on a heatproof plate and warm them in a microwave oven on medium-high power for 2 minutes. If you don't have a microwave oven (and you can't borrow your neighbour's!), place the stuffed bitter gourds snugly in a frying pan, slit side up, on medium heat. Stir the gourds gently from side to side for a few minutes, but do not turn them upside down. Add ¼ cup of water. It will steam right away, and this steam will further heat the gourds. When the water has evaporated, in 1 to 2 minutes, cover the pan and heat for another minute so that the potato masala gets warmed as well. Uncover and serve.

TO SERVE Arrange 2 stuffed gourds on each individual plate. Serve immediately.

VEGETABLE KOFTES WITH CREAMY TOMATO CURRY

KOFTES

1 pound celery root, peeled, OR celery stalks

1 pound sweet potatoes, peeled

1 pound carrots

1 pound Yukon Gold or red potatoes, unpeeled

1 ½ tablespoons + 1 teaspoon salt

1 cup chopped cilantro

1 tablespoon finely chopped jalapeño pepper (or to taste)

½ cup corn flour

½ cup chickpea flour

3 tablespoons ground coriander

2 tablespoons Garam Masala (page 23)

1 tablespoon ground cumin

cooking oil for deep-frying

This rich, creamy vegetarian dish is popular with everyone, including many meat lovers. In the summer of 2013, we made dinner for the Indian ambassador to the United States and his staff, and his favourite dish of the meal was this curry.

The two vegetables you must use in this dish are the carrots and potatoes. Aside from those, you can use whatever root vegetables are in season. If you can't find celery root, you can use celery in its place. Celery root has a more "root vegetable" flavour and is slightly smoother in taste than celery. Also keep in mind that how much cinnamon and cloves you use will depend on the strength of their aroma. Too much will ruin the curry, and not enough will not give it the depth of flavours. Our measurements are based on strongly scented spices. And be generous with the garlic.

Although this recipe makes 32 to 36 koftes, you will need only 18 of them to serve six people. Koftes are not hard to make but they do take time, so we make a large batch and freeze half of them in a resealable plastic bag. They will keep frozen for up to 3 months. Thaw frozen koftes before mixing them with the curry and heating everything through together. The curry recipe makes enough for six, so double the recipe if you are serving a crowd. Serve this recipe with any pilaf or flatbread.

SERVES 6 (MAKES 32 TO 36 KOFTES)
PREP & COOKING TIME: 2 HOURS

KOFTES Wash and wipe dry all vegetables. In a food processor fitted with the grating disc or using a box grater, grate each vegetable separately. Combine the grated vegetables in a large bowl, add the 1 teaspoon of salt and allow the mixture to stand at room temperature for 30 minutes.

Have ready a second large bowl. Working over the sink, scoop a handful of the grated vegetables into your hand and squeeze the mixture between your palms to remove any excess water. Place the "dried" vegetables in the second bowl. Repeat with the remaining grated vegetables.

Have ready a baking sheet. To the grated vegetables add the cilantro, jalapeños, corn flour, chickpea flour, coriander, garam masala, cumin and the 1 ½ tablespoons of salt; mix until thoroughly combined. Scoop ¼ cup or just slightly less of the mixture into your hands and roll it between your palms to form a mini sausage, about 2 inches long and 1 inch wide. (If the grated vegetables are not easily sticking together, mix in an additional ⅓ cup of chickpea flour.) Set the kofta on the baking sheet. Repeat with the remaining mixture until you have 32 to 36 koftes.

Line a baking sheet with paper towels. Heat 4 inches of oil in a deep-sided pot on medium-high heat for 5 minutes. To check if the oil is hot enough, gently drop a teaspoonful of the kofta mixture into the oil. If it rises immediately and starts to cook, the oil is hot enough. Using a slotted spoon, gently drop the koftes into the hot oil and cook for 2 to 3 minutes, or until they are golden. You do not want to overcrowd the pot, so fry them in batches, if necessary. Transfer the koftes to the paper towel–lined baking sheet. Set aside while you prepare the curry.

CREAMY TOMATO CURRY Heat the oil in a wide, heavy-bottomed pot on medium-high heat. Add the onions and sauté for 8 to 10 minutes, or until browned but not blackened. Stir in the garlic and sauté for another 3 minutes, or until the garlic is light gold and the onions are a slightly darker brown. Stir in the ginger and tomatoes, then reduce the heat to medium. Add the cinnamon stick, cloves, cumin, coriander, turmeric, cayenne and salt. Stir well and sauté this masala for 5 minutes, or until the oil glistens on the tomatoes.

Pour in the water and stir well. (This step prevents the cream from splitting when you add it.) Pour in the cream, stir well and cook the curry for 10 to 15 minutes, or until it is gently boiling. Stir in the green fenugreek leaves, mixing well so the mixture does not clump. Turn off the heat if you are not ready to serve the koftes immediately. While it's hard to find the cloves, you can remove the cinnamon stick if you wish.

CREAMY TOMATO CURRY

½ cup cooking oil

2 cups finely chopped onions (1 large)

3 tablespoons finely chopped garlic (9 to 12 medium cloves)

2 tablespoons finely chopped ginger

2 cups puréed fresh or canned tomatoes (5 to 6 medium)

½ stick cinnamon

6 to 9 whole cloves

1 ½ tablespoons ground cumin

1 ½ tablespoons ground coriander

2 teaspoons turmeric

1 teaspoon ground cayenne pepper

2 teaspoons salt

3 cups water

2 cups whipping cream

1 ½ tablespoons dried green fenugreek leaves

continued...

TO SERVE Add the koftes to the creamy tomato curry and heat on medium heat for 20 minutes, allowing the mixture to boil gently. The koftes will become soft as they heat and they will absorb the flavours of the curry. Divide the curry among individual bowls, ensuring 2 to 3 koftes per serving.

SUGGESTED PAIRINGS

SPROUTED LENTIL, BELL PEPPER AND CARROT SALAD (PAGE 129)

CAULIFLOWER AND POTATO IN TOMATO MASALA (PAGE 111)

NAPA CABBAGE IN TOMATO MASALA SALAD (PAGE 59)

GRAINS

AND

LEGUMES

THE TRADITION OF GRAINS

Whether eating grains and legumes is good for our health is currently a popular conversation in North American food circles. Our personal opinion is that unless you have severe allergies to these foods, whole grains and legumes are a valuable source of protein, iron and fibre to complement or replace meat in our diet. Indians have been eating grains and legumes for generations, and we know from the accumulated wisdom of our ancestors that these foods keep our arteries, as well as our guts, clean, which actually helps to prevent heart disease and high blood pressure.

Daal roti is India's national staple dish. This meal of lentils and chapatti (flatbread made traditionally from whole-wheat and bran flours) is considered a basic human right, even during war and poverty. During the violence and displacement that surrounded Indian partition in 1947, all refugee families were given rations of chapatti flour and yellow lentils. Even today, many Indians, including the kitchen staff in all our restaurants, *choose* to eat lentils and chapattis for lunch at least two or three days a week. In most cases, this is not a choice made for health reasons, but because a lot of us—including those of us who now eat meat—grew up eating lentils, beans and chapattis every day of our childhoods. We like the taste and texture of these foods with our vegetables and meats, and they connect us with our culture and our community.

We realize that not all flours are nutritious. Both at home and in our restaurant kitchens, we make the distinction between whole grains and processed grains. Naan is made from processed all-purpose flour, and we reserve this bread only for special occasions. Nor do we eat the more refined white Basmati rice every day. Whenever possible, we choose heartier whole-wheat flatbreads or brown rice and pair them with a variety of lentils, chickpeas or dried beans prepared in many different ways. Here are some of our non-traditional yet Indian-spiced recipes, including several options that are gluten free. Try these on their own for a vegetarian meal or pair them with meat dishes to enhance the flavour and help your digestion.

SPROUTED LENTIL, BELL PEPPER AND CARROT SALAD

Indians don't really eat salad in the same way as North Americans and Europeans, but it is rare for there not to be a crunchy side dish alongside a meal, even if it's just sliced onions marinated in salt and lemon. In our family that means, at the very least, chopped cucumbers and green bell peppers tossed in some salt and lemon juice.

Although this vegan and gluten-free recipe contains no specifically Indian ingredients, it can be described as an Indian salad. To make it really Indian, you can always add 1 teaspoon of black salt! To add a bit of non-Indian, stir in 2 tablespoons of extra-virgin olive oil. Indians prefer the salty tartness of lemon or lime juice to balance out the spices in the Indian dishes that accompany a salad, but if you are eating this salad on its own, include the olive oil, as it softens the lemon.

Serve this chilled salad alongside Raita (page 33) as an accompaniment to any meal or as a light meal or snack on its own.

SERVES 6
PREP TIME: 30 MINUTES (NOT INCLUDING SPROUTING TIME)

IN A LARGE bowl or a salad bowl, combine the lentils, carrots, bell peppers, green onions, celery, lemon juice, salt and olive oil (if using). Stir well and refrigerate until ready to serve.

TO SERVE Stir in the cilantro and serve immediately.

SUGGESTED PAIRINGS
ANY OF OUR MAIN DISHES

2 cups Sprouted Lentils (page 42)

2 to 3 carrots, chopped

1 to 2 bell peppers (any colour), chopped

3 green onions, white and green parts, finely chopped

1 cup diced celery (optional)

juice from 1 very juicy lemon

½ tablespoon salt OR ½ teaspoon salt + 1 teaspoon black salt

2 tablespoons extra-virgin olive oil (optional)

½ to ¾ cup chopped cilantro

QUINOA AND CAULIFLOWER SALAD

4 cups water

2 cups white quinoa, rinsed

2 ½ teaspoons salt

¼ cup grapeseed or olive oil

1 teaspoon cumin seeds

12 to 16 fresh curry leaves (optional)

1 teaspoon turmeric

1 head cauliflower, cut into 1- to 2-inch pieces, including stems

⅔ cup chopped cilantro

⅔ cup chopped green onions, white and green parts

¼ cup lemon juice

Quinoa has become the new kale, the new super-healthy food that everyone is eating. It is a very nutritious—high in protein and amino acids—and versatile food, and we enjoy it in a side salad or rolled into chapattis as a sandwich filling. When we introduced this salad to the Vij's and Rangoli menus, it was more popular with our staff (who ate big bowls of it every day) than with our customers. This surprised us, considering how many food writers and customers asked what gluten-free and healthy options we had on our menu. It turns out that when our customers splurged on a dinner out, they wanted heavily curried foods with naan, rice and chapattis, not this light and refreshing salad, which reminded them of meals at home. Unfortunately we cannot justify a high food cost for staff meals only (organic quinoa is expensive), so we took this dish off our menu while we thought over the "quinoa dilemma."

During this time of dilemma, Meeru learned about how quinoa's popularity was affecting its price and availability. Global demand for quinoa was making it too expensive for people in Peru and Bolivia, where it is an ages-old nourishing staple food, to buy. And it was putting pressure on farmers in these countries to grow only quinoa and to grow more than their soils could reasonably support. Quinoa was pushing out plant diversity and depleting the nutrients in the soil. For the umpteenth time over one of our Sunday night dinners, Meeru talked about how binge eating the same foods (bananas, kale, meat, quinoa …) leads to environmental problems. In return, Vikram quipped: "So, it's okay in the Meeru world that my father binge eats yellow lentils and chapatti, but it's not okay for Canadians to binge eat quinoa? You binge drink coffee every morning."

It took us two years to resolve this question, but this lovely quinoa salad is now back on the menu, and it's popular with both staff *and* customers. We support eating lentils or beans—or both— every day, but different kinds from different parts of the world. (Vikram's father's daily lentil curry is part of Meeru's "grandfather clause".) And we now serve smaller portions of this dish alongside other salads.

continued...

This salad is ingredient specific, and we don't suggest any substitutes because this is simply the best combination. We use only grapeseed or olive oil and do not recommend ghee or coconut oil, as these fats solidify when they cool and taste too heavy with this light salad. In addition to the florets, we also cut up and add the stems of the cauliflower, since they are just as healthy and delicious. You can serve this salad warm or cooled.

SERVES 10 TO 12

PREP & COOKING TIME: 45 MINUTES

IN A MEDIUM pot, combine the water, quinoa and 1 teaspoon of the salt. Bring to a boil on high heat. Reduce the heat to a simmer, cover and cook for 15 minutes. Turn off the heat and allow to stand, covered, for 5 minutes. Transfer to a salad bowl and set aside.

While the quinoa is cooking, heat the oil in a medium pot or frying pan on medium heat for 3 to 4 minutes. Add the cumin seeds and allow them to slowly and gently sizzle for 15 seconds. If you are using the curry leaves, add them now and stir well for 1 minute. Add the turmeric and the 1 ½ teaspoons of salt and cook for 1 minute. Stir in the cauliflower, tossing it gently with the spices so that it is completely yellow from the turmeric, and sauté for 10 to 15 minutes, stirring regularly, or until it is cooked al dente. Add the cilantro, green onions and lemon juice and stir well.

Stir the hot cauliflower and all the spices into the bowl of quinoa. Mix well until combined.

TO SERVE Serve family style at the table or in individual bowls as a side salad.

SUGGESTED PAIRINGS

GRILLED SPICY TILAPIA WITH LIGHT COCONUT-TOMATO CURRY (PAGE 173)

EGGPLANT, KALE AND CAULIFLOWER CURRY (PAGE 88)

GREEN AND BLACK CARDAMOM CREAM CHICKEN CURRY (PAGE 194)

GOLDEN BEET, WHEAT BERRY AND SPROUTED LENTIL SALAD WITH VIJ'S DRESSING

This beautiful salad is healthy *and* flavourful, and we designed it specifically as a sophisticated side dish to accompany our Vij's mains. However, it's also a wonderful dinner party salad that's not limited to accompanying just Indian dishes. Although it's easy to make, because of the number of ingredients this salad is labour intensive and does require a few steps, so make a big batch all at once, as it will keep refrigerated in an airtight container for up to a week. The key ingredients are the beets, wheat berries and sprouted lentils, but we often substitute equal amounts of carrots, corn and/ or steamed (and cooled) asparagus instead of the green beans.

Wheat berries have a wonderful nutty flavour and a crunchy texture. They are full of vitamins and fibre and are much less expensive than farro, though you can use an equal amount of farro in place of the wheat berries if you prefer it. You can buy high-quality frozen cooked wheat berries at some grocery stores, which is what we do at home. At Vij's, we buy bulk wheat berries and soak them for six to eight hours in triple the amount of water. To cook them, we place the wheat berries and their soaking water in a pot, bring it to a boil, reduce the heat to low, cover and simmer for 50 minutes, or until the wheat berries are crunchy on the outside but soft inside.

The key spices for the dressing are the fennel seeds and green cardamom. You do not roast the cardamom seeds, but it's important to dry-roast the fennel seeds in a small frying pan on medium heat for a few minutes and then grind them to get rid of any grassy texture. Ground dried ginger, known as *sund*, has a very different flavour from fresh ginger and is available from Indian grocers. In our experience, the ground ginger found on supermarket spice shelves also has a different taste from *sund*. Although the rest of the spices are optional, the more you include, the more depth of flavour in the dressing. Serve this salad as a side to any main dish.

2 cups Sprouted Lentils (page 42)

2 cups cooked wheat berries

1 pound green beans, cooked and chopped into ½-inch pieces

1 pound raw golden beets, peeled and cut into thin slivers

¾ cup fresh lemon juice

¾ cup honey

2 tablespoons roasted and ground fennel seeds

1 teaspoon ground green cardamom seeds (discard the pods)

1 teaspoon ground ginger (optional)

½ teaspoon ground cloves

½ teaspoon ground kalonji seeds

2 teaspoon salt

1 teaspoon ground black pepper

SERVES 10

PREP TIME: 45 MINUTES (NOT INCLUDING SPROUTING THE LENTILS AND COOKING THE WHEAT BERRIES) + 2 HOURS TO MARINATE

continued…

IN A LARGE salad bowl, combine all the ingredients and mix together really well. Refrigerate the salad, covered, for at least 2 hours. The salad will keep for up to a week.

TO SERVE Stir well and pass around the bowl.

SUGGESTED PAIRINGS
VEGETABLE KOFTES WITH CREAMY TOMATO CURRY,
IF YOU HAVE ALL DAY TO COOK (PAGE 122)
ASSORTED MUSHROOMS AND WINTER SQUASH CURRY (PAGE 100)
OVEN-BAKED CHICKEN WITH CHARD AND RED RADISHES (PAGE 186)

SPICY RICE PILAF FOR LOCAL VEGETABLES

1 ½ cups Basmati rice

2 ⅔ cups water

⅓ cup + 1 teaspoon cooking oil

1 cup chopped green onions, white and green parts

1 cup chopped fresh tomatoes (2 to 3 medium)

1 tablespoon finely chopped jalapeño pepper

1 tablespoon ground cumin

½ teaspoon ground cayenne pepper

½ teaspoon ground fenugreek seeds

½ tablespoon ground black mustard seeds

2 teaspoons salt

1 to 2 cups cooked chickpeas and/or pinto beans (canned is fine) and/or chopped bell peppers, asparagus, cabbage, kale, cauliflower, eggplant, corn, etc.

1 cup (6 to 7 ounces) cubed Paneer (page 38) (optional)

1 sprig fresh mint, leaves only, chopped

½ cup chopped fresh cilantro

We always have a basic rice pilaf on the menu at our restaurants, but it changes as local vegetables come and go through the late spring and summer. This spicy rice pilaf is a perfect background to most local vegetables, legumes and paneer. If you want to add, for example, chickpeas, you can stir them straight into the hot rice. If you want to add vegetables, we recommend that you sauté them separately in a small amount of oil or ghee to add a crunchy texture, but you can also steam them and stir them into the pilaf. Do not add more than 1 cup of paneer cubes, otherwise your pilaf will be too rich. Try combining a cup of paneer with a cup of peas or chopped mushrooms. For an extra health kick, use 1 cup chopped dandelion greens in place of the cilantro. Serve the pilaf on its own, with Yogurt (page 34) or with curry dishes.

SERVES 6 AS A MEAL OR 8 AS A SIDE
PREP & COOKING TIME: 1 HOUR

PLACE THE RICE in a medium pot. Wash the rice well under cold water and drain. Repeat the washing and draining once more. Add the 2 ⅔ cups water to the rice and allow to soak for 40 minutes.

While the rice is soaking, heat the ⅓ cup of oil in a heavy-bottomed frying pan on medium-high heat. Add the green onions and sauté for 1 minute. Stir in the tomatoes, jalapeños, cumin, cayenne, fenugreek, mustard seeds and 1 ½ teaspoons of the salt; cook for 4 to 5 minutes. Add the legumes and/or chopped vegetables, adding the ones that need the most cooking time first, and continue stirring until cooked through (cauliflower will take 10 minutes while bell peppers or asparagus take a few minutes). Stir in the paneer, turn off the heat, and allow to rest for 5 minutes. Stir in the fresh mint and cilantro. Set aside.

Add the 1 teaspoon of oil and ½ teaspoon of the salt to the rice. Bring to a boil on high heat. Reduce the heat to a simmer, cover and cook for 12 minutes. Turn off the heat, but *do not* remove the lid. Allow the rice to rest, covered, for another 5 minutes.

Combine the hot rice with the cooked legumes and/or vegetables and/or paneer.

TO SERVE Gently scoop the pilaf into a large bowl and serve family style.

SUGGESTED PAIRINGS
COCONUT JAPANESE-INDIAN GREEN BEAN CURRY (PAGE 98)
GRILLED SQUASH WITH SUGAR-ROASTED BEETS AND CUMIN-SPICED
ONIONS (PAGE 108)
VEGETABLE KOFTES WITH CREAMY TOMATO CURRY (PAGE 122)

BROWN RICE AND YELLOW CHANNA DAAL PILAF

BROWN RICE AND CHANNA DAAL PILAF

3 ounces dried porcini mushrooms

8 cups very hot tap water

2 cups brown Basmati rice

2 cups channa daal

½ tablespoon salt

1 teaspoon coconut oil

PUMPKIN SEED AND ONION MASALA

⅓ cup + 2 tablespoons coconut oil

2 cups chopped fresh tomatoes (5 to 6 medium)

2 tablespoons mild ancho chili powder

1 large onion, cut in half lengthwise and thinly sliced

1 cup pumpkin seeds or sunflower seeds

1 tablespoon ground cumin

1 teaspoon salt

1 teaspoon ground yellow mustard seeds

½ tablespoon crushed cayenne pepper

¾ teaspoon ground fenugreek seeds

Most Indians do not grow up eating brown rice, and so they much prefer the taste and texture of white Basmati. Vikram is one of these people, as are our kitchen staff at Vij's and Rangoli. Somewhat surprisingly, though, this is the favourite rice pilaf of our kitchen staff. The best part of this dish is that it's super healthy and vegan without even trying to be. The porcini mushroom broth is crucial to this pilaf's rich flavour.

For this recipe, you will need to find *channa daal* (daal means "lentil"). Although they are actually baby chickpeas that have been split and polished, they look like yellow split peas and are sometimes mislabelled "yellow split pea lentils." You can buy channa daal at any Indian grocer. We also prefer to use pumpkin seeds in this masala for their distinct flavour, but sunflower seeds work equally well. The key is to sauté the seeds with the onions for 1 to 2 minutes on as high a heat as possible without burning them. This ensures their crispiness.

This recipe comes together in four easy steps. To save time, rinse your rice and lentils while the mushrooms are soaking and prepare your masala while the rice and lentils are cooking. If we have any leftover masala, we use it as a topping for anything, including tofu or steak. It is also delicious over hearty white bread that's been spread with Boursin or ricotta cheese. Leftover masala will keep, refrigerated in an airtight container, for up to a week.

SERVES 8
PREP & COOKING TIME: 1 HOUR

BROWN RICE AND CHANNA DAAL PILAF Place the porcini mushrooms in a medium bowl, add the hot water and allow to soak for 30 minutes.

While the mushrooms are soaking, combine the brown rice and channa daal in a medium bowl, wash them well under cold water and drain. Repeat the washing and draining once more. Transfer the rice and daal to a large pot. Slice the onions for the masala.

Place a fine-mesh sieve over the pot with the rice and daal. Pour the mushrooms and their broth into the sieve. Chop the porcini mushrooms and set aside.

Add the salt and coconut oil to the rice mixture and bring to a boil on high heat. Stir once, reduce the heat to a simmer, cover and cook for 50 minutes. Carefully remove the lid and taste a spoonful of rice and daal to see if they are tender. If not, cover and allow them to simmer for another 5 minutes. Turn off the heat.

PUMPKIN SEED AND ONION MASALA While the rice and daal are simmering, in a small frying pan, combine the 2 tablespoons of oil, the tomatoes and the ancho chili powder. Cook on high heat, stirring regularly, for 3 to 4 minutes, or until the tomatoes become a purée and the oil glistens on top. Set aside until the pilaf is cooked, then stir this tomato mixture into the pilaf.

In a large frying pan, heat the ⅓ cup of coconut oil on high heat for 1 minute. Add the onions (enjoy the sizzling noise!) and sauté for 6 to 8 minutes, or until the edges are dark brown and the middle is light golden. Add the pumpkin (or sunflower) seeds and cook, stirring constantly, for 2 minutes. The seeds are cooked when you hear a slight popping sound; they will also become darker and the edges will brown. Reduce the heat to medium and immediately add the cumin, salt, mustard seeds, cayenne and fenugreek. Stir and sauté this masala for 2 to 3 minutes. (If your spices are pre-roasted, 2 minutes is enough. If they are store-bought and pre-ground, they will need 3 minutes.) If the bottom of the pan is turning black, add 1 teaspoon more of the oil or reduce the heat. When the spices are cooked, turn off the heat and stir in the chopped porcini mushrooms. Continue to stir the mushrooms for 2 minutes (they will cook in the heat of the hot masala).

TO SERVE Scoop the pilaf onto a large platter and serve it family style in the middle of the table. Either top the pilaf with the pumpkin seed and onion masala or pour the masala into a serving bowl and allow your guests to help themselves.

SUGGESTED PAIRINGS
CHICKEN AND LOCAL VEGETABLE CURRY (PAGE 188)
ROASTED SPICY OKRA WITH WALNUTS AND JELLY BEANS (PAGE 94)
SAUTÉED BRUSSELS SPROUTS SALAD (PAGE 90)

LENTIL AND BASMATI RICE PILAF
WITH FRIED EGGS

2 cups white Basmati rice

7 ½ cups water

2 teaspoons salt

⅓ cup + 1 teaspoon ghee or cooking oil + more for frying the eggs

⅔ cup masur lentils

⅔ cup washed mung lentils

1 to 2 teaspoons chopped ginger

1 teaspoon turmeric

¼ teaspoon asafoetida (optional)

2 teaspoons cumin seeds

1 cup finely chopped onions (1 medium-large)

1 cup chopped tomatoes (2 to 3 medium)

1 teaspoon crushed cayenne pepper

½ cup chopped cilantro

6 to 16 eggs (1 or 2 per serving)

2 cups Sprouted Lentils (page 42)

kimchee to taste

Our family loves Korean food. One of our favourite dishes is *bibimbap*, which means "mixed rice," and combines warm white rice topped with sautéed vegetables, hot chili paste, soy sauce and often an egg and sliced meats. The ingredients are stirred together and served with kimchee. This recipe is our vegetarian Indian version, which Meeru affectionately calls Lentil Curry Bippim Bap, and it has become a favourite in our family and among our friends. Since this is an Indian dish, we serve the kimchee on the side, but if you enjoy this spicy fermented condiment, be sure to spoon some on top of your finished pilaf.

In this multi-faceted dish, we pair soft (read: mushy) lentils with crunchy sprouted mung lentils. You will need two varieties, both of which are very fast cooking: masur lentils (split red lentils), which are available from just about any grocery store, and washed yellow mung (or moong) lentils (split and washed mung beans, which Vikram's father eats every night!), which are sold at South Asian grocers. Both are considered staple lentils for lighter daily meals. Meeru's family is a strict masur family, and Vikram's family is a strict washed mung family. Of course, both families make these lentils with lots of turmeric and ginger. While both lentils are light, the mung dissolves very quickly when cooked. We now combine half and half, but you can use just one or the other. Serve this dish with some Napa Cabbage in Tomato Masala Salad (page 59) on the side.

SERVES 6 TO 8

PREP & COOKING TIME: 45 MINUTES

PLACE THE RICE in a medium bowl, wash well under cold water and drain. Repeat the washing and draining once more. Combine the rice with 3 ½ cups of the water in a large pot and allow it to soak for 40 minutes.

Add 1 teaspoon of the salt and the 1 teaspoon of ghee (or oil) to the rice and bring to a boil on high heat. Reduce the heat to a simmer, cover and cook for 12 minutes. Turn off the heat and

continued...

allow the rice to sit, covered, for 5 minutes. Stir the rice gently and then cover again and set aside.

Combine the masur and mung lentils in a medium bowl, wash well under cold water and drain. Repeat the washing and draining once more. Combine the lentils with 4 cups of the water in a large pot. Add the ginger, turmeric, asafoetida and 1 teaspoon of the salt. Bring to a boil on medium-high heat and allow it to boil for a few minutes. Use a small fine-mesh sieve or a spoon to skim off the foam that rises from the lentils. (This step prevents the lentils from boiling over once you cover them.) Reduce the heat to low, cover and cook the lentils for 15 minutes. Turn off the heat, stir, cover again and set aside.

While the lentils are cooking, make the masala. In a medium frying pan, heat the ⅓ cup of ghee (or oil) on high heat for 1 minute. Add the cumin seeds and allow them to sizzle for 15 seconds. Add the onions and sauté for 8 to 10 minutes, or until uniformly dark brown—but not black. Stir in the tomatoes and cayenne and sauté for 2 to 3 minutes, or until the oil glistens on the tomatoes. Stir this masala into the pot of cooked lentils. Be sure to get all of the masala stuck on the sides of the frying pan by swirling some of the lentils in the frying pan and pouring them back into the pot. Stir in the cilantro. Keep warm over low heat.

Have ready a large platter. Place the frying pan you used for the masala on medium-high heat. Add about 2 teaspoons ghee (or oil) per egg and and crack 3 to 4 eggs into the pan. Cook, sunny side up, for 3 to 5 minutes, until the whites are cooked through but the yolks are still runny. Transfer them to the platter. Repeat with the remaining eggs.

TO SERVE On a serving platter or on individual plates, arrange a layer of rice. Pour the hot lentil curry over the rice and top with the fried eggs. Sprinkle with sprouted lentils. Serve kimchee either on top of the sprouted lentils or in a side dish so everyone can help themselves. Serve immediately.

SWEET AND SAVOURY MILLET PILAF WITH FENNEL SEEDS

This sweet and savoury combination is extraordinary. It is rich, yet full of nutrition and fibre and easy to digest. Although we created this recipe as a vegan and, while we were at it, gluten-free dessert, our customers didn't order it. But Meeru was adamant about how delicious it was and transferred it from the dessert menu to the dinner menu. At Vij's, we now serve this pilaf with Chicken and Local Vegetable Curry (page 188) as an appetizer. A good, high-quality sugar is the key to this recipe. Indian raw sugar is known as *gur*, and your best option is to buy some high-quality Indian raw sugar or demerara sugar. Do not confuse Indian raw sugar with the cheaper chunks of palm sugar that are often sold as raw sugar. Usually, raw sugar is more golden and doesn't appear as dry and old as palm sugar. The same goes for demerara—be sure to buy real demerara and not the cheaper golden sugars made from molasses. If you reheat this dish, place it on low to medium heat, uncovered, and stir gently and regularly, so the millet doesn't clump together.

SERVES 8 (½ CUP PER PERSON)
PREP & COOKING TIME: 20 MINUTES

4 cups water

2 cups millet

½ teaspoon salt

1 ½ tablespoons ghee or coconut oil

1 teaspoon fennel seeds

1 cup raw sugar or demerara sugar

½ teaspoon ground cayenne pepper (optional)

whipped cream (optional, if serving as dessert)

SUGGESTED PAIRINGS
CHICKEN AND LOCAL VEGETABLE CURRY (PAGE 188)
LAMB POPSICLES WITH GARLIC AND RICOTTA-FENUGREEK TOPPING (PAGE 218)
COCONUT PRAWN CURRY (PAGE 168)

BRING THE WATER to a boil in a medium pot on high heat. Stir in the millet and the salt. Reduce the heat to a simmer, cover and cook the millet for 15 minutes. Turn off the heat and allow the millet to sit, covered, for 5 minutes. Stir the millet and set aside.

While the millet is cooking, melt the ghee (or coconut oil) in a small frying pan on medium-high heat. Add the fennel seeds and cook, stirring regularly, until they begin to sizzle, in about 4 minutes. Allow them to sizzle for 30 seconds. Stir in the sugar and cayenne.

TO SERVE Stir the sugar-fennel mixture into the cooked millet and scoop it into a large serving bowl or individual bowls. Serve immediately.

MILLET AND BELL PEPPER PILAF

1 ½ cups millet

3 ½ cups water

⅓ cup cooking oil

2 cups finely chopped onions (1 large)

2 tablespoons chopped ginger

1 tablespoon ground yellow mustard seeds

2 teaspoons paprika (not smoked paprika)

1 teaspoon ground fenugreek seeds

1 teaspoon ground cayenne pepper

1 teaspoon salt

2 small red and/or green bell peppers, chopped into ½-inch cubes

SUGGESTED PAIRINGS
CREAMY YAM CURRY (PAGE 104)
PORK TENDERLOIN WITH HOCK IN YELLOW MUSTARD SEED AND CREAM CURRY (PAGE 214)
STEAMED SALMON OR ARCTIC CHAR WITH CAULIFLOWER CURRY (PAGE 174)

Historically, millet, which is known as *bhajra* in India, was considered peasant food—a grain for people who didn't have enough money to buy Basmati rice. Nevertheless, it has always been considered healthy, and when an already healthy Indian vegetarian wanted to go "light" and cleanse their system, they would make their chapatti out of ground millet. It has not been eaten for pleasure. In our Vij's kitchen, we always know that our head cook, Amarjeet Gill, is on some sort of a health kick or diet when we start getting our chapattis made from bhajra flour.

While "gluten free" is not a known phrase in India, millet is gaining popularity in North America as a gluten-free option. In India as well, millet is becoming more popular. Like quinoa, millet is light, healthy and easy to cook. Whereas quinoa has a slightly bitter (yet pleasant) corn-like taste, millet is nutty in flavour. And whereas quinoa gets lost in meat curries, this millet pilaf carries itself with a punch, especially for those who are gluten free but not vegetarian.

SERVES 6
PREP & COOKING TIME: 30 MINUTES

COMBINE THE MILLET AND WATER in a medium pot and bring to a boil on high heat. Reduce the heat to low, stir, cover and cook for 15 minutes. Turn off the heat and stir again, then cover and set aside for 5 minutes. (We find that this resting period makes the millet more flaky than sticky.)

While the millet is cooking, heat the oil in a medium frying pan on medium-high heat. Add the onions and sauté for 6 minutes, or until light golden. Stir in the ginger and sauté for 1 minute. Add the mustard seeds, paprika, fenugreek, cayenne and salt; sauté for 1 ½ to 2 minutes. Stir in the bell peppers and cook for 2 minutes, until softened but not discoloured. Remove from the heat.

TO SERVE Spoon the millet into a large bowl, stir in the bell pepper mixture and serve immediately, family style.

CARROT AND SEMOLINA CREPES

11 ounces carrots, grated

2 cups semolina

½ cup finely chopped cilantro

2 tablespoons ground coriander

2 teaspoons salt

1 teaspoon chopped ginger (optional)

½ teaspoon ground cayenne pepper (optional)

2 cups water

1 ⅓ cups buttermilk (3.25% milk fat)

6 tablespoons ghee or coconut oil

On a visit to her maternal grandparents in Virginia many years ago, a three-year-old Nanaki told her grandmother that she didn't like carrots. An Indian not liking carrots? Omi shot Meeru a glance that said she'd committed a parenting sin. Whereas carrots in India are small, red and super sweet, North American carrots are huge and less flavourful, but that doesn't stop many Indians from eating them. One of Vikram's father's favourites, for example, is carrots lightly spiced in cumin, ginger and turmeric. The next evening, Omi served a carrot and semolina crepe as part of dinner. All of us, including Nanaki, devoured this crepe, though Nanaki and Shanik very sneakily spit out the tiny pieces of ginger and gave them to Meeru. At the end of the meal, Meeru's mother commented smugly, "Even though they're American carrots, they're organic and they're healthy, so you have to figure out a way to make them taste good."

Semolina is basically cream of wheat cereal, but you can now find organic semolina at many stores as well. We use ghee or coconut oil in this recipe to give the crepes a nice crispy exterior with a bit of extra flavour. And we use buttermilk because we like its rich yet tangy flavour, but you can use water instead. Crepes made with water won't be quite as rich but they'll be crispier. Either way, you'll have a thick, carrot-heavy batter, which you'll need to spread a bit like frosting on the griddle or crepe pan. Use an offset spatula and try to keep the thickness consistent so the crepes cook evenly. You can also make smaller crepes, if you have a smaller appetite or if you find them easier to manage in the pan. These crepes also make for a great savoury breakfast or brunch. You can adjust the spice level according to your preference. When we make these with Nanaki and Shanik, we keep the spicing at a minimum and use only the coriander and cilantro. When we make them for adults only, we add the ginger and cayenne, and serve the crepes with lemon or mango pickle on the side.

These crepes are best eaten as soon as they come off the stove, one by one, while they're hot and crispy. At home, everyone sits down to eat and we have one or two designated "crepe makers" who bring the hot crepes to the table. In fact, in India this is how

continued...

many families traditionally eat their flatbreads—the father and children sit down at the table and eat while the mother prepares piping-hot chapattis or *paranthas* and serves them one by one. Meeru and Vikram have fond memories of sitting at the dinner table with our fathers while our mothers brought out such hot chapattis that we could barely touch them. When we were younger, our fathers (it was specifically their job) would break our chapattis in half for us so they would cool faster. This was our daily breaking of bread as a family. And our mothers always knew what we were talking about at the table and never hesitated to participate in the conversations while they were making and serving chapattis. Once all the chapattis were cooked, our moms would sit down with us for dinner. We never left the table until Mom had finished eating.

SERVES 6 (1 LARGE CREPE PER PERSON)
PREP & COOKING TIME: 45 MINUTES

TO SERVE Serve immediately on individual plates.

SUGGESTED PAIRINGS
DATE CHUTNEY (PAGE 28)
LEMON PICKLE (PAGE 29)
RAITA (PAGE 33)

COMBINE THE CARROTS, semolina, cilantro, coriander, salt, ginger, cayenne, water and buttermilk in a large bowl. Stir well and allow the mixture to sit for 15 minutes. The semolina will swell a bit.

Heat your griddle or crepe pan on high heat. Melt 1 tablespoon of ghee (or coconut oil) on the griddle. To test that the oil is hot enough, drop a teaspoonful of the batter onto the pan. If it starts to sizzle immediately, the oil is ready.

Reduce the heat to medium, ladle ⅔ cup of the batter onto the griddle and using a spatula, spread it into a circle 10 to 11 inches in diameter and an even thickness. Cook for 4 minutes, or until the crepe has dried considerably. Using a spatula, carefully turn the crepe over and cook it for 4 minutes more. (If you prefer a crispier crepe, cook each side for 30 seconds longer.) Transfer the cooked crepe to a plate and serve immediately. Repeat with the remaining oil and batter.

YELLOW LENTIL CURRY WITH BLACK LENTIL MASALA

If you eat as many lentils as Indians do—and our family eats a lot!—you easily discern and appreciate even mild flavour differences between various types of lentils. So we like to vary the yellow lentils we use in this dish. In our efforts to eat different types of lentils from different parts of the world, we came up with this dish for lentils that are grown in North America rather than in India. We suggest Sunrise red (they cook yellow with the turmeric) or Shasta yellow lentils for their slightly firmer texture and milder flavour, but you can use any yellow or orange lentil for this curry as long as you cook them just until tender. Most yellow lentils take about 20 to 30 minutes, except for channa daal, which takes 45 to 50 minutes.

We also mix some black "caviar" lentils into this recipe. Not only do the yellow and black look beautiful together, but each lentil provides a different layer of flavour. Be sure to use the faster-cooking black caviar lentils (also called beluga lentils) instead of black urad daal, which must be soaked overnight and boiled for an hour minimum. Although most yellow lentils tend to disintegrate a bit while cooking, black lentils will keep their shape if they are not overcooked. Therefore, we do not cook the black lentils in an abundance of water. Eat this curry like a soup, with bread on the side.

SERVES 6 TO 8

PREP & COOKING TIME: 45 MINUTES

SUNRISE YELLOW LENTIL CURRY Place the yellow and black lentils in 2 separate bowls. Separately, wash both lentils well under cold water and drain. Repeat the washing and draining once more.

In a medium pot, combine the yellow lentils, 4 cups of the water, 1 teaspoon of the salt and the ginger and turmeric. In a smaller pot, combine the black lentils with the remaining 1 ¾ cups of water and ½ teaspoon of salt. Bring both pots to a boil, uncovered, on high heat. Once boiling, reduce the heat to a simmer, partially cover and cook for 20 to 25 minutes. Both sets of lentils should be tender.

Drain any excess water from the black lentils. Stir the cilantro stems into the yellow lentils.

SUNRISE YELLOW LENTIL CURRY

1 ½ cups Sunrise or other yellow lentils

¾ cup black caviar lentils

5 ¾ cups water

1 ½ teaspoons salt

½ tablespoon chopped ginger

1 teaspoon turmeric

2 tablespoons very finely chopped cilantro, stems only (optional)

BLACK LENTIL MASALA

⅓ cup cooking oil

1 cup finely chopped onions (1 medium-large)

½ cup puréed fresh or canned tomatoes

1 tablespoon Garam Masala (page 23) OR ground cumin

1 teaspoon ground cayenne pepper

½ teaspoon salt

continued...

BLACK LENTIL MASALA While the lentils are cooking, make your masala. Heat the oil in a frying pan on high heat for 1 minute. Add the onions and sauté for 6 to 8 minutes, or until dark around the edges but not burned. Stir in the tomatoes and reduce the heat to medium. Add the garam masala (or cumin), cayenne and salt and stir well. Cook for 3 to 4 minutes, or until the oil glistens on the tomatoes. Turn off the heat and gently stir in the black lentils. Season to taste with more salt, if necessary.

TO SERVE Divide the piping-hot yellow lentils evenly among large soup bowls. Dollop 2 to 3 tablespoonfuls of the black lentil masala in the middle of each serving. Serve immediately.

SUGGESTED PAIRINGS

**STEAMED SALMON OR ARCTIC CHAR WITH
CAULIFLOWER CURRY (PAGE 174)**

**NAPA CABBAGE IN TOMATO MASALA SALAD, FOR A LIGHT YET
COMPLETE MEAL (PAGE 59)**

SPICY RICE PILAF FOR LOCAL VEGETABLES (PAGE 136)

CHICKPEA AND SPROUTED LENTIL CAKES

4 cups cooked or drained canned chickpeas

¼ to ⅓ cup cooking oil + ¾ cup for pan-frying

1 cup finely chopped onions (1 medium-large)

1 cup puréed fresh or canned tomatoes (2 to 3 medium)

1 tablespoon salt

1 tablespoon ground cumin

1 tablespoon ground coriander

1 teaspoon turmeric

½ teaspoon ground cayenne pepper

1 ½ cups Sprouted Lentils (page 42)

7 to 8 tablespoons rice flour

These savoury cakes are great for a dinner party, either as an appetizer or as a vegetarian main course. Although they are fried, they are healthy and full of fibre. At Rangoli, we use this recipe as a filling for samosas, but samosas are difficult, messy and time-consuming to make at home. If you are comfortable using store-bought filo pastry, you can wrap portions of this filling in layers of filo brushed with oil, ghee or melted butter and bake them in the oven, as you would spanakopita or other filled filo pastries. These filo bundles make a nice appetizer. Easier still is the recipe we've given here, in which the "filling" is formed into cakes and lightly pan-fried in oil. Serve them as a hearty vegan appetizer with some Date Chutney (page 28), or for non-vegans, with Sour Cream Dressing (page 27). Or turn these cakes into a full dinner by serving them alongside any hot curry. For a vegan dinner, serve them with the vegan version of the Bengali-style Curry (page 36).

You can prepare the ingredients a day or two in advance and pan-fry the cakes just before serving, or freeze the cooked cakes and thaw and reheat them in a 325°F oven for 15 minutes before serving. The chickpea-lentil masala is already cooked by the time you fry the cakes, so pan-fry them just enough to crisp up the outside. And don't worry about forming perfect circles, as these cakes look more tempting when they are roughly shaped.

SERVES 8 TO 10 (MAKES 24 TO 30 CAKES)
PREP & COOKING TIME: 1 HOUR

IN A FOOD PROCESSOR, pulse the chickpeas just until they are roughly chopped and hold together. (You want them to be textured, not a smooth paste like hummus.) Set aside.

Heat the ¼ cup of oil in a medium pot on medium-high heat for 1 minute. Add the onions and sauté for 8 to 10 minutes, or until browned. Stir in the tomatoes and then add the salt, cumin, coriander, turmeric and cayenne. Cook for 5 minutes, or until the oil glistens on the tomatoes. Stir in the chopped chickpeas and the sprouted lentils. Transfer the mixture to a large bowl and allow to cool.

Have ready a large baking sheet or cutting board. When you are ready to fry the cakes, stir 7 tablespoons of the rice flour into the chickpea mixture until well combined. The mixture should stick together enough to form cakes. If it does not, stir in the remaining 1 tablespoon of rice flour. Scoop about ¼ cup of the chickpea mixture into your hand. Form the mixture into a cake that is 2 ½ inches in diameter and about 1 inch thick. Set the chickpea-lentil cake on the baking sheet. Repeat with the remaining batter. (You should have 24 to 30 cakes.)

Line another baking sheet with paper towels. Heat ½ inch of oil in a large frying pan on high heat for 3 to 4 minutes. To test if the oil is hot enough, carefully place 1 cake in the pan. If it sizzles immediately, the oil is ready. Arrange as many cakes in the pan as will fit with space to turn them (cook in batches, if necessary) and fry for 2 minutes per side, or until lightly browned. Transfer the cakes to the paper towel–lined baking sheet to drain.

TO SERVE Arrange the cooked cakes on a large serving platter and serve warm.

SUGGESTED PAIRINGS
BENGALI-STYLE CURRY (PAGE 36)
CREAMY YAM CURRY (PAGE 104)
EGGPLANT, KALE AND CAULIFLOWER CURRY (PAGE 88)

GREENS SAUTÉED IN BROWN SUGAR AND TURMERIC WITH CHICKPEAS IN TAMARIND CURRY

SAUTÉED GREENS

⅓ cup cooking oil

1 tablespoon cumin seeds

2 tablespoons finely chopped garlic (6 to 7 medium cloves)

1 tablespoon finely chopped jalapeño pepper

1 tablespoon finely chopped ginger

1 teaspoon turmeric

1 to 1 ½ teaspoons salt

½ cup regular dark brown sugar

16 ounces chopped greens (leaves only)

CHICKPEAS IN TAMARIND CURRY

⅓ cup cooking oil

2 cups finely chopped onions (1 large)

12 to 16 fresh curry leaves

1 ½ tablespoons Garam Masala (page 23) OR ground cumin

1 teaspoon salt

½ teaspoon ground black pepper

3 tablespoons Tamarind Paste (page 26)

¼ cup water

3 cups cooked chickpeas, drained

Greens and chickpeas are a natural combination with Indian spices. In this recipe, you can use just one green or a combination of kale, collards, beet greens, mizuna and mustard greens. The only green that doesn't work is spinach, because of its soft texture. While the greens provide a slightly bitter flavour and the sugar a mild sweetness, the tamarind contributes a lovely tartness that complements the sweet. Make your own Tamarind Paste (page 26) or buy it from any Asian grocer or gourmet food store. Just be sure you're buying pure tamarind with no added sugars. It should have the consistency of thick applesauce. If your paste is runny, you may need to add an extra tablespoon.

Any leftovers will keep refrigerated for up to a week. Spread the leftovers on your favourite flatbread, roll it up as a wrap and top with Yogurt (page 34). You can eat either curry separately as well.

SERVES 6
PREP & COOKING TIME: 45 MINUTES

SAUTÉED GREENS In a medium-large, heavy-bottomed pot, heat the oil on medium-high heat. Sprinkle in the cumin seeds and allow them to sizzle for 20 seconds. Stir in the garlic and sauté for 3 minutes, or until golden. Add the jalapeños and ginger, stir well and cook for 1 minute. Add the turmeric and salt and sauté for 1 minute more. Stir in the brown sugar, followed by the greens. Mix well to ensure the greens are well coated in the spice "masala." Continue cooking, stirring constantly, for 4 minutes, or until the greens are wilted. Cover and cook for 1 minute. Turn off the heat and allow the greens to sit, covered, for at least 5 minutes to allow the spices to suffuse into the greens and the greens to soften further.

CHICKPEAS IN TAMARIND CURRY In a medium-large, heavy-bottomed pot, combine the oil and onions on medium-high heat and sauté for 8 to 10 minutes, or until browned. (The darker you can get the onions the better, but don't let them burn.) Add the curry leaves and reduce the heat to medium. Stir in the garam masala (or cumin), salt and black pepper and sauté for 2 to 3 minutes, stirring continuously. Mix in the tamarind paste, water and chickpeas. Reduce the heat to low, cover and cook for up to 10 minutes to allow the flavours to blend and the masala and the chickpeas to warm through.

TO SERVE Mix the greens well. Arrange an equal amount in the centre of individual shallow bowls. Spoon about ½ cup of the chickpeas in tamarind curry over each serving of greens. Serve immediately.

SUGGESTED PAIRINGS
"ETHIOPIAN FLAG" BASMATI RICE PILAF, WITH OR WITHOUT THE LAMB SHANK (PAGE 221)
CAULIFLOWER AND POTATO IN TOMATO MASALA (PAGE 111)
LAMB POPSICLES WITH GARLIC AND RICOTTA-FENUGREEK TOPPING (PAGE 218)

LENTIL CURRY WITH SAUTÉED EGGPLANT, POTATOES AND FENNEL

1 pound eggplant, cut into 1-inch cubes

3 ½ teaspoons salt

1 ½ cups masur or washed mung lentils (see page 140)

8 cups water

1 stalk celery, cut into large pieces

1-inch-square piece of ginger, cut into 4 large pieces

⅓ cup butter or ghee

1 cup finely chopped red onions (1 medium-large)

1 bulb fresh fennel, trimmed and sliced

1 cup chopped fresh, juicy tomatoes (2 to 3 medium)

1 tablespoon ground coriander

1 pound Yukon Gold potatoes, unpeeled, cut into 1-inch cubes

1 teaspoon ground black pepper

1 cup chopped cilantro, stems included

½ tablespoon crushed cayenne pepper

This pretty, healthy dish showcases coriander and cilantro—the seed and the leaves of the same plant. It also showcases fresh fennel. Don't worry about the size of your fennel bulb—it can be small or large, as this vegetable is mild in flavour. And don't forget to use the oval belly button trick (page 84) when you buy your eggplants.

You can use yellow washed mung lentils, orange masur lentils or Sunrise red lentils for this recipe. The yellow and orange ones cook faster, and the orange ones are the easiest to find in most grocery stores (where they are called red lentils).

SERVES 6 TO 8

PREP & COOKING TIME: 1 TO 1 ½ HOURS, DEPENDING ON HOW LONG YOU SALT THE EGGPLANT

PLACE THE eggplant in a medium bowl and, using your hands, rub 1 ½ teaspoons of the salt into the flesh. Transfer the eggplant to a colander and set in the sink to drain for 30 minutes to 1 hour. (This step draws the moisture out of the eggplant and tenderizes the flesh.)

When you are ready to cook the eggplant, place a clean tea towel on the counter. Rinse the eggplant quickly under cold water to get out any excess salt. Shake off the water and place the rinsed eggplant on the tea towel. Gently blot the eggplant. You don't need to wipe each piece separately; you just don't want to cook with soggy eggplant.

Place the lentils in a medium bowl, wash well under cold water and drain. Repeat the washing and draining once more. In a large pot, combine the lentils with the 8 cups water, 2 teaspoons of the salt, the celery and the ginger. Bring to a boil, uncovered, on high heat. Reduce the heat to medium-low and partially cover so the lentils don't boil over. Cook mung or masur lentils for 20 minutes, Sunrise lentils for 30 minutes.

While the lentils are cooking, melt the butter (or ghee) in a medium to large heavy-bottomed pot on medium-low heat. Add the onions and sauté for 10 minutes, or until translucent and very slightly browned on the edges. Increase the heat to medium, add the fennel and sauté for 5 minutes. Increase the heat slightly and stir in the tomatoes and coriander. Cook for 3 minutes. Reduce the heat to medium-low, stir in the potatoes and cook, stirring regularly with a wooden spoon (be sure to keep scraping the bottom of the pot so nothing burns), for 10 minutes. Add the eggplant and cook for 5 minutes. Poke a small knife into the potatoes to see if they are cooked through. If so, stir in the pepper, cilantro and cayenne.

TO SERVE Divide the lentil curry evenly among individual bowls. Top with the eggplant, potatoes and fennel.

SUGGESTED PAIRINGS
SIMPLE GRILLED CHICKEN WITH OPTIONAL SPICE SPRINKLE (PAGE 190)
BROWN RICE AND YELLOW CHANNA DAAL PILAF (PAGE 138)
BEEF SHORT RIBS IN KALONJI AND CREAM CURRY (PAGE 208)

NAVY BEANS IN EGG AND TOMATO MASALA

⅓ cup cooking oil

½ tablespoon black mustard seeds

2 cups finely chopped onions
(1 large)

2 tablespoons chopped ginger

1 ½ cups puréed fresh or canned
tomatoes (5 medium)

1 ½ tablespoons ground cumin

1 teaspoon turmeric

1 teaspoon ground cayenne
pepper

1 teaspoon ground fenugreek
seeds

1 teaspoon salt

1 cup whipping cream

1 large egg

3 cups cooked navy beans

6 ounces spinach, including stems,
chopped

SUGGESTED PAIRINGS
**CLAY POT SAFFRON CHICKEN AND
RICE (PAGE 198)**
**GRILLED SPICY TILAPIA WITH LIGHT
COCONUT-TOMATO CURRY
(PAGE 173)**
**EGGPLANT, KALE AND CAULIFLOWER
CURRY (PAGE 88)**

At Vij's, we serve this dish on various fish or chicken dishes. You can just as easily serve these beans on toast or slices of baguette or as part of a vegetarian meal. If you do serve them on toast (English style), then you could also fry an egg separately and place it on top of the beans.

This recipe is designed for the mild-flavoured white navy (or Great Northern) bean, and we do not recommend that you substitute other beans or lentils. We prefer to soak 1 ½ cups of dried beans overnight and then boil them in 4 cups of water until tender, about 40 minutes. Or we put the unsoaked beans in a pressure cooker with 4 cups water and cook at full pressure for about 15 minutes. You can also use canned navy beans, though they have a slightly mushy texture.

SERVES 4 AS A MEAL OR 8 AS A SIDE
PREP & COOKING TIME: 45 MINUTES

HEAT THE OIL in a medium pot on high heat for 1 minute. Sprinkle in the mustard seeds and allow them to sizzle for 15 seconds, or until you hear a popping sound. (The seeds pop when they start to burn, but a few popping sounds is usual.) Add the onions, reduce the heat to medium-high and sauté for 8 to 10 minutes, or until dark brown but not burned. Add the ginger, tomatoes, cumin, turmeric, cayenne, fenugreek and salt; sauté for 5 minutes, or until the oil glistens on the tomatoes. Reduce the heat to low.

In a small bowl, gently whisk together the cream and egg. Stir this mixture into the tomato masala until well combined and cook for 1 minute. Add the navy beans, stir well and cook for 3 minutes, or until heated through. Stir in the spinach and cook for 1 minute.

TO SERVE Spoon the beans and masala into a large serving bowl and serve family style.

BROWN BASMATI RICE, PINTO BEAN AND VEGETABLE "CAMPER'S CURRY"

After eating lunch at Rangoli, one of our regular customers was at the till buying ten bags of our packaged curries, which can be reheated in a saucepan, microwaved or boiled in the bag at home. Meeru asked him if there was a special reason for buying so many, and he replied that he and his friends were heading out for four days of heavy-duty hiking in the local mountains and that they'd be eating these meals for dinner while camping overnight. (Meeru has hiked, but her day hikes end with a bed at home or in a hotel room, so eating more than the basics while hiking or camping had never occurred to her.) Surprisingly, these readymade meals are a favourite of many Vancouver campers.

When Meeru discovered this customer was buying only meat curries because he found them the most filling, she got to work on creating an energy-packed vegetarian curry. This hearty all-in-one rice and curry dish is known as our "camper's curry" because it was specifically designed to fill up hungry campers. Of course, you don't need to go camping to enjoy this risotto-like curried pilaf. The brown rice and pinto beans are filling and therefore the key components, but once you've made this dish according to our recipe, feel free to substitute other beans or vegetables. Brown rice is healthier and takes longer to digest than white, which makes it good, filling camping food, but you can substitute white rice here. A nice addition to this curry is 6 to 8 chopped dates and ½ cup of Spiced Pumpkin Seeds (page 40). Sprinkle them on top if you're serving this curry at home or mix them into the heated curry once you've warmed it on your camp stove. And if you're at home, Raita (page 33) is also a great accompaniment.

SERVES 6 TO 8

PREP & COOKING TIME: 1 HOUR

PLACE THE RICE in a medium bowl, wash it well under cold water and drain. Repeat the washing and draining once more. In a medium pot, combine the rice, the 1 tablespoon of oil, 1 teaspoon

2 cups brown Basmati rice

⅓ cup + 1 tablespoon cooking oil

2 teaspoons salt

6 cups water

1 large red onion, sliced

1 tablespoon finely chopped ginger (optional)

1 teaspoon finely chopped jalapeño pepper (or to taste)

2 cups puréed fresh or canned tomatoes (5 to 6 medium)

1 tablespoon ground cumin

1 tablespoon mild ancho chili powder

1 teaspoon turmeric

1 teaspoon crushed cayenne pepper

¼ to ½ teaspoon ground cinnamon OR 1 whole stick

1 pound green beans, chopped, OR green peas

2 to 3 red bell peppers, sliced lengthwise

2 cans (each 14 ounces) pinto beans, drained, OR 2 ½ cups cooked beans

continued...

of the salt and 5 cups of the water. Bring to a boil on high heat, reduce the heat to a simmer, cover and cook for 50 minutes. Carefully remove the lid (avoid the steam) and check the rice. If it's not fully cooked, cover and continue cooking for 10 minutes or so. Once cooked, turn off the heat.

While the rice is cooking, make the masala. Heat the ⅓ cup of oil in a medium pot on medium-high heat for 1 minute. Add the onions and sauté for 8 minutes, or until golden. Stir in the ginger and jalapeños and sauté for 1 minute. Add the tomatoes, cumin, ancho chili powder, turmeric, cayenne, cinnamon and 1 teaspoon of the salt. Stir well and cook for 5 minutes, or until the oil glistens on the tomatoes. Add the 1 cup water, green beans (or green peas), bell peppers and pinto beans; stir well. Bring to a boil, reduce the heat to low, cover and cook for 5 minutes. Turn off the heat. Remove the cinnamon stick.

TO SERVE Scoop the rice into a large serving bowl, top with the masala and stir well to combine. Serve immediately.

SUGGESTED PAIRINGS
MILDLY CURRIED BEEF SHORT RIBS (PAGE 211)
SAUTÉED BRUSSELS SPROUTS SALAD (PAGE 90)
EGGPLANT IN THICK YOGURT AND GARLIC CURRY WITH BATTERED
FRIED ONIONS (PAGE 84)

BENGALI-STYLE BLACK BEAN AND CORN CURRY

⅓ cup cooking oil

1 teaspoon cumin seeds

1 tablespoon ground panch poran

1 bunch green onions, white and green parts, chopped

2 cups puréed fresh or canned tomatoes (5 to 6 medium)

2 teaspoons salt

1 teaspoon turmeric

1 teaspoon ground cayenne pepper

1 cup whipping cream

1 cup water

1 pound fresh or frozen corn kernels

3 cans (each 14 ounces) black beans OR 3 ½ to 4 cups cooked black beans

This black bean and corn curry is about as close to an Indian vegetarian chili as we can get. Fresh corn cut off the cob and blanched quickly has the best flavour and texture, but we use frozen organic corn when fresh is not available. Canned black beans can be very mushy, so we suggest that you cook your own. Rinse and drain 1 ½ cups of dried beans, soak them in 5 cups water for 6 to 8 hours and then boil them, covered, in their soaking water until tender, 35 to 45 minutes. Or cook the unsoaked beans in 4 cups of water in a pressure cooker at full pressure for about 10 minutes. If you do use canned beans, be sure to rinse them thoroughly in a colander. And if you use canned beans with salt, use ½ teaspoon less salt in this recipe. Serve this curry with any rice pilaf.

SERVES 6

PREP & COOKING TIME: 35 TO 40 MINUTES

HEAT THE OIL in a large pot on high heat for 1 minute. Sprinkle in the cumin seeds and allow them to sizzle for 20 seconds, or until darker. Sprinkle in the panch poran and allow the spice to sizzle and foam for 5 seconds. Add the green onions, stir well and sauté for 2 minutes. Stir in the tomatoes and reduce the heat to medium. Add the salt, turmeric and cayenne, stir well, and cook the masala for 4 to 5 minutes, or until the oil glistens on the tomatoes.

Pour the whipping cream into a medium bowl. Mix about 2 tablespoons of the hot masala into the cream. (This step prevents the cream from splitting when it is mixed into the hot curry.) Pour the mixture into the pot. Pour the cup of water into the bowl that held the cream and stir. Empty this water into the pot. Stir in the corn and black beans, increase the heat to high and bring to a boil. Cover, reduce the heat to low and simmer for 5 minutes.

TO SERVE Pour the curry into a large serving bowl and serve family style.

SUGGESTED PAIRINGS

QUINOA AND CAULIFLOWER SALAD (PAGE 130)

CARROT AND SEMOLINA CREPES (PAGE 146)

ZUCCHINI, SQUASH AND POTATO SAUTÉ (PAGE 106)

SEAFOOD

HEALTHY AND SUSTAINABLE SEAFOOD

Our family's seafood consumption has noticeably decreased in the past five years—not because we don't enjoy seafood (especially prawns), but because we no longer eat unhealthy farmed or endangered fish at restaurants, and neither do we purchase fish from any grocery stores that cannot tell us where it comes from. The cheaper the fish on any menu or at any store, the more likely that it is "dirty" fish that has been raised and harvested unsustainably. We prefer to eat healthy seafood—which does cost more money—a few times a month instead of cheap seafood more often. This way, we can truly appreciate and enjoy our seafood dinners.

This change was hardest for Vikram, who loves seafood as much as he loves meat. It's not easy to eat less of something that you can afford and that seems to be readily available, and to eat less for the sake of "climate change" that does not seem to be affecting your life today. What we are noticing, though, is that it's becoming more and more difficult to find sustainable and clean sources of fish that aren't bad for human health. The levels of mercury (a heavy metal that can cause neurological damage) that basically come from carbon dioxide pollution in the water are getting very high, especially in larger wild fish. Farm-raised fish are not always better: many of the enclosed fish farms are overcrowded, which leads to high levels of feces in the water. The water must then be cleaned with chemicals and the fish treated with antibiotics to protect them against disease. Like animals raised on factory farms, the fish in these overcrowded fish farms are often fed waste products too.

Having said that, there is great hope that with more consumer demand for sustainable seafood, sustainable aquaculture will continue to rise in popularity and take some of the pressure off fishing. Currently, three-quarters of the world's fish stock is in decline because of overfishing, yet world consumption of seafood—and demand for cheap seafood—remains unnecessarily high. The reality is that our waters are being rapidly depleted of life, and no life in the oceans will eventually mean no life on this planet, at least as we know it today. Instead of feeling cynical and hopeless about this possibility, we are firm believers that the choices we make as a family and in our restaurants are more useful and positive than not making any changes because the larger system is so

screwed up anyway. If even fifty people read this and make changes, for us that is fifty more people than before. When there is less demand for cheap fish, there will be less overfishing and less unsustainable fish farming.

Both Canada and the European Union have created organic guidelines and certification programs for aquaculture. And when making our seafood choices at home and in our restaurants, we follow the Monterey Bay Aquarium's Seafood Watch program. We also follow the Vancouver Aquarium's Ocean Wise program, and we cross-reference the lists to ensure that our choices are recommended on both. We read many journals on this topic in order to stay current on new practices, good and bad. Most important, we always ask at markets and restaurants: "Where is the fish from and is it sustainable?" And we keep asking, from the cashier on up to the manager and the fisher, until we get an answer. After all, it was a food writer, almost fifteen years ago, asking one of our servers whether the orange roughy on our menu was an endangered fish that got us started on this journey.

COCONUT PRAWN CURRY

⅓ cup coconut oil

1 tablespoon cumin seeds

4 bunches green onions, green and white parts, chopped

3 tablespoons chopped garlic (9 medium cloves)

2 cups chopped fresh, juicy tomatoes (5 to 6 medium)

½ tablespoon salt

1 teaspoon crushed cayenne pepper

2 cups unsweetened desiccated shredded coconut

1 cup water

1 tablespoon dried green fenugreek leaves

36 to 42 prawns, peeled and deveined

SUGGESTED PAIRINGS
**EGGPLANT IN THICK YOGURT AND
GARLIC CURRY WITH BATTERED
FRIED ONIONS—BUT ONLY IF
YOU'RE A GARLIC LOVER (PAGE 84)**
**COCONUT JAPANESE-INDIAN GREEN
BEAN CURRY (PAGE 98)**
**CHICKPEA AND SPROUTED LENTIL
CAKES (PAGE 152)**

Thank goodness for the abundance of coconut prawn curries in this world. If you enjoy these two ingredients, you can never get enough of this combination.

Although "tiger" prawns from Asian countries are relatively inexpensive and widely available in grocery stores, they are on the "avoid" list of many sustainable-seafood organizations. We recommend that you review the "best choices" on the Monterey Bay and Ocean Wise sustainable-seafood lists before buying your prawns.

If you are vegetarian or do not have prawns on hand, the tomato-coconut masala is delicious on its own, served over brown or white rice. It also makes a great chutney or sandwich spread. Or you can substitute an equal amount of chickpeas for the prawns. The first time you make this curry, follow our measurements. Once you've tasted this version, feel free to add as much garlic, coconut and green onions as you like.

SERVES 6
PREP & COOKING TIME: 30 MINUTES

HEAT THE coconut oil in a medium saucepan on medium-high heat for 1 minute. Add the cumin seeds and allow them to sizzle for 15 seconds. Stir in the green onions and sauté for 4 to 6 minutes, or until gold on the edges. Add the garlic and sauté for 3 minutes, or until golden. Stir in the tomatoes, salt and cayenne, reduce the heat to medium and sauté the masala for 5 minutes. Stir in the coconut and cook for 5 minutes, or until the coconut has softened. Pour in the water and add the fenugreek leaves, then stir and bring the mixture to a gentle boil.

Stir the prawns into the gently boiling masala, cover and cook for 3 to 5 minutes, or until they turn pink. Overcooked prawns become chewy and lose their subtle flavour, so check the prawns after 3 minutes. If they are not cooked, cover and check them again every minute. As soon as they turn pink, remove the pot from the heat.

TO SERVE Pour the prawn curry into a large bowl to serve family style, or divide the curry (and prawns) evenly among individual bowls. Serve immediately.

MARINATED SPOT PRAWNS WITH MASHED ROASTED EGGPLANT

ROASTED EGGPLANT

1 pound eggplant

1 cup finely chopped green onions, green and white parts

½ cup chopped cilantro

1 tablespoon salt

1 teaspoon ground black pepper

1 cup chopped fresh tomatoes (2 to 3 medium)

⅓ cup lemon juice

PRAWN MASALA

1 pound prawns (about 24), peeled

½ teaspoon ground cayenne pepper

½ teaspoon salt

¼ cup (or less) + ⅓ cup cooking oil

1 tablespoon cumin seeds

1 teaspoon turmeric

½ tablespoon chopped jalapeño pepper (or to taste)

1 cup chopped fresh tomatoes (2 to 3 medium)

GRILLED BELL PEPPERS

1 pound red bell peppers (4 medium or 3 large), cut in quarters or sixths

In the summer of 2015, the Vancouver Farmers Markets created an online marketplace called the Food Hub to bring together British Columbia farmers' products and restaurants. The farmers posted photos of their produce online so customers could see the size and quality, then restaurants placed their orders. If they bought in bulk, they saved money. If enough restaurants in the area placed large enough orders, the Hub arranged for the delivery of this produce to the restaurants once or twice a week. For Vij's and Rangoli restaurants, this system worked wonderfully—and the beautiful local eggplants we received were the inspiration for this dish.

The Food Hub orders became a highlight in our restaurants. When our Vij's head cooks, Amarjeet and Sital, were sitting behind Meeru's laptop selecting the produce from the website, all the kitchen cooks would crowd around to see the photos and prices of the produce. (Most of our kitchen staff have their own summer vegetable gardens and they love to compare prices.) And when the Food Hub delivery arrived, Amarjeet would receive the produce at the Vij's kitchen and deliver half of it to the Rangoli kitchen next door. When the first orders of eggplant arrived, Amarjeet held out one of these deep purple globes for everyone to admire. The eggplant was half the size of the ones you buy in the grocery store, but it was picture perfect. As she walked over to Rangoli, several kitchen staff followed. "Is it just a beautiful face with no personality?" someone asked. Our Rangoli kitchen manager, Raj Samra, sliced it in half. This beautiful eggplant did not disappoint: it had tons of personality—hardly any seeds inside, just creamy white flesh. In other words, it had what we call in Hindi/Punjabi *meettas*, an abundance of flavour.

At Vij's we serve this dish as a stand-alone feature appetizer, and the spices in this recipe are deliberately light because fresh seasonal eggplant and British Columbia spot prawns are so sweet in early summer that you don't want to hide their flavour. Grilling bell peppers brings out their *meettas* and complements the eggplant and prawns. However, don't worry if you don't have these exact ingredients or if it's no longer summertime. Substitute larger globe eggplant, other sustainably raised prawns and even yellow or green bell peppers. Just make sure to serve equal amounts of the dish's three parts to everyone. If you have a gas stove, roast the eggplant directly over the flame; if not, use a barbecue or outdoor grill instead. You can grill the bell peppers on the barbecue, too, or in the oven, if you prefer.

SERVES 6 TO 8

PREP & COOKING TIME: 1 HOUR

ROASTED EGGPLANT To roast your eggplant on a gas stove-top, turn on the exhaust fan. Place the eggplant directly on the element and turn the flame to high. Using a pair of heatproof tongs, rotate the eggplant every 3 to 4 minutes for 20 to 30 minutes. It will make sizzling noises, then begin to soften and wilt. Once the eggplant has completely wilted and you think that you won't be able to turn it over any more (you will), it's roasted. Transfer to a bowl to cool.

To grill the eggplant on a barbecue or outdoor grill, place the eggplant directly on the grill and turn the heat to high. Using a pair of heatproof tongs, rotate the eggplant every 3 to 4 minutes until completely wilted, 20 to 30 minutes. Transfer to a bowl to cool.

Holding the eggplant over the bowl (in case it slips from your hands), run cold water over the skin for 10 seconds. Using your fingers, peel off and discard as much of the burned skin as possible. Place the peeled eggplant in a clean bowl and mash it roughly with a fork (or chop it finely). Add the green onions, cilantro, salt, black pepper, tomatoes and lemon juice. Mix well and set aside.

PRAWN MASALA Place the prawns in a large bowl. Add the cayenne, salt and the ¼ cup of oil, and using your hands, mix gently until well combined. Cover and refrigerate until you are ready to cook them.

In a pan large enough to hold all the prawns in a single layer,

continued...

heat the ⅓ cup of oil on medium-high heat for 1 minute. Add the cumin seeds and allow them to sizzle for 15 seconds. Stir in the turmeric, jalapeños and tomatoes and sauté for 2 minutes. Turn off the heat.

GRILLED BELL PEPPERS To grill the bell peppers on the barbecue or outdoor grill, turn the grill to high. Place the slices of bell peppers directly on the grill and heat each side for 30 to 45 seconds, until lightly grilled but not charred. Transfer the cooked peppers to a plate.

To grill them in the oven, place the oven rack in the top of your oven. Preheat the oven to 450°F. Line a baking sheet with aluminum foil. Arrange the slices of bell pepper, skin side down, on the foil. Bake for 45 seconds. Poke with the tip of a knife. If the peppers are still very raw, cook for another 45 seconds. The peppers should be firm enough to hold the eggplant and prawns.

FINISH PRAWN MASALA Heat the prawn masala on medium heat for 1 minute. Stir in the marinated prawns and cook, stirring regularly, for 3 to 5 minutes, or until the prawns are pinkish orange and firm but still soft. Remove from the heat.

TO SERVE Arrange the bell peppers, skin side down, on a serving tray. Tuck 2 tablespoons of the eggplant into each bell pepper, then divide the prawns and masala evenly over each slice of bell pepper. Serve family style.

SUGGESTED PAIRINGS
BROWN RICE AND YELLOW CHANNA DAAL PILAF (PAGE 138)
YELLOW LENTIL CURRY WITH BLACK LENTIL MASALA (PAGE 149)
CREAMY YAM CURRY (PAGE 104)

GRILLED SPICY TILAPIA WITH LIGHT COCONUT-TOMATO CURRY

Tilapia sometimes gets a bad rap from chefs for having little taste and being a "cheap" fish. But it is a great match for stronger Indian spices. Unlike other, softer white fish, tilapia can be grilled easily without breaking. And, it's a sustainable fish. Buy the tilapia cut into pieces, large or small, whichever you prefer for handling and serving.

To keep the focus on the flavours, we serve this spice-rubbed fish at Rangoli with a light coconut curry that uses most of the same spices. The ginger in the curry complements the ajwain seeds in the fish rub. Too much ajwain can ruin the dish, but just enough adds a wonderful and original touch to the fish. If you do not have any of this spice, don't worry, you will still enjoy this dish.

SERVES 6
PREP & COOKING TIME: 45 MINUTES + 2 TO 6 HOURS TO MARINATE

GRILLED TILAPIA Have ready a large baking sheet. In a large bowl, combine the oil, mustard seeds, cumin, salt, ajwain and cayenne; mix well. Add the tilapia, tossing it gently to coat the fish on all sides with as much of the oil and spices as possible. Spread out the fish in a single layer on the baking sheet, cover and refrigerate for 2 to 6 hours.

COCONUT-TOMATO CURRY Melt the coconut oil in a medium pot on medium heat. Add the tomatoes, ginger and jalapeños and stir. Add the mustard seeds, cumin, turmeric and salt; sauté for 5 minutes, or until the oil glistens on top of the tomatoes. Stir in the coconut milk and water. Increase the heat to medium-high and bring the mixture to a boil. Cover, reduce the heat to low and simmer for 10 minutes, or until the oil glistens on top of the curry.

FINISH TILAPIA Heat a barbecue or stovetop grill to medium-high. Place the tilapia skin side down on the grill and cook for 3 to 4 minutes per side, or until the fish flakes easily when poked gently with a knife.

TO SERVE Divide the tilapia evenly among 6 individual bowls. Pour the curry around the tilapia and serve immediately.

GRILLED TILAPIA

⅓ cup cooking oil

1 tablespoon ground black mustard seeds

1 tablespoon ground cumin

½ tablespoon salt

1 teaspoon ajwain seeds

1 teaspoon ground cayenne pepper

2 pounds boneless tilapia, skin on, cut into 5- to 6-ounce pieces or smaller 2- to 3-ounce pieces

COCONUT-TOMATO CURRY

¼ cup coconut oil

1 cup puréed fresh or canned tomatoes (2 to 3 medium)

1 tablespoon chopped ginger (or to taste)

1 teaspoon chopped jalapeño pepper

½ tablespoon ground black mustard seeds

½ tablespoon ground cumin

1 teaspoon turmeric

1 teaspoon salt

2 cups premium full-fat coconut milk, stirred

2 cups water

SUGGESTED PAIRINGS
CREAMY FENUGREEK AND CUMIN POTATOES (PAGE 96)
CREAMY YAM CURRY (PAGE 104)
NAPA CABBAGE IN TOMATO MASALA SALAD (PAGE 59)

STEAMED SALMON OR ARCTIC CHAR
WITH CAULIFLOWER CURRY

STEAMED SALMON (OR ARCTIC CHAR)

¼ cup cooking oil

½ tablespoon mild ancho chili powder

1 teaspoon ground cayenne pepper

1 teaspoon salt

1 ½ pounds salmon or arctic char fillets, skin on, cut into 2 ½-inch cubes

CAULIFLOWER CURRY

⅓ to ½ cup cooking oil

1 ½ cups finely chopped red onions (1 large)

1 tablespoon finely chopped fresh ginger

⅔ cup puréed fresh or canned tomatoes

3 whole star anise

1 ½ tablespoons ground cumin

½ tablespoon salt

1 teaspoon turmeric

1 teaspoon ground cayenne pepper

⅓ cup full-fat plain yogurt, stirred

3 cups water

1 medium head cauliflower, cut into 1-inch florets

½ cup chopped cilantro (optional)

We make this recipe with either wild Pacific salmon or farmed arctic char. There are many varieties of salmon, but we prefer the chinook (also known as king salmon or spring salmon) for its combination of meaty taste and high fat content. And although we find that some farmed fish—even a few varieties selected as "best choice" options by the sustainable-seafood advocates—are lacking in flavour and texture, we do love farmed arctic char. It is lighter in flavour and more affordable than salmon, and it is delicious.

Salmon is best served very simply. And since Indian spices and "simple" don't combine easily, it can be hard to use salmon in an Indian dish—especially when turmeric and salmon don't match well. The secret is to keep the salmon simple and add the spices to the cauliflower. Think of the cauliflower as the perfect mediator between the salmon and the spices; it allows these two adversaries to become best friends in this dish and carry out the most interesting conversation.

In our view, steaming the fish in this recipe makes the spices and the taste of the fish stand out more. You must, however, use the oil in the marinade, otherwise the spices will not cook properly while they are steaming. (If you prefer, you can sear the fish in a frying pan on medium heat for 3 to 4 minutes per side instead of steaming it.) Serve bread or rice on the side.

SERVES 6

PREP & COOKING TIME: 1 HOUR + 2 TO 3 HOURS TO MARINATE

STEAMED SALMON (OR ARCTIC CHAR) In a large bowl, combine the oil, ancho chili powder, cayenne and salt. Add the salmon (or arctic char), mixing it gently to coat the fish on all sides. Cover and refrigerate for 2 to 3 hours.

CAULIFLOWER CURRY Heat the oil in a large, heavy-bottomed frying pan on medium-high heat for 1 minute. Add the onions and sauté for 8 minutes, or until golden. Stir in the ginger and sauté for 30 seconds. Add the tomatoes, star anise, cumin, salt, turmeric and cayenne; stir well and sauté for 4 to 5 minutes, or until the oil glistens on the tomatoes. Turn off the heat.

Place the yogurt in a small bowl. Add 2 to 3 tablespoons of the tomato masala to the yogurt and mix well. (This step prevents the yogurt from splitting when it is mixed into the hot masala.) Stir the yogurt into the masala, scraping all of the yogurt from the bowl with a spatula. Stir in the water, turn on the heat to medium-high and bring to a boil, stirring gently and regularly.

Carefully add the cauliflower, cover, reduce the heat to low and simmer for 5 minutes, or until the cauliflower is tender but not overcooked. (Cauliflower releases lots of water when it is over-cooked, and this will dilute the curry as well as causing the cauliflower to become mushy and lose its own flavour.) Remove the lid and stir in the cilantro. Turn off the heat until ready to serve. You can stir through the cauliflower curry and take out the star anise at this time, or you can let your guests know to expect them.

FINISH FISH Have ready a baking sheet. Pour 1 to 1 ½ inches of water into a large pot with a steamer insert and bring to a boil on high heat. Place the salmon (or arctic char) in the steamer, making sure that the pieces do not overlap. (Cook the fish in batches, if necessary.) Reduce the heat to medium-high, place the steamer over the boiling water, cover and steam for 5 minutes, or until the fish flakes easily when poked gently with a knife. Using a slotted spoon, transfer the fish to the baking sheet.

TO SERVE If necessary, reheat the cauliflower curry on high heat until it just begins to boil, about 5 minutes. Stir and immediately turn off the heat. Divide the fish equally among 6 large dinner bowls, heaping it in the middle of the bowl. Ladle the cauliflower curry around the fish. Serve immediately.

SUGGESTED PAIRINGS
BROWN RICE AND YELLOW CHANNA DAAL PILAF (PAGE 138)
GRILLED SQUASH WITH SUGAR-ROASTED BEETS AND
CUMIN-SPICED ONIONS (PAGE 108)
SPROUTED LENTIL, BELL PEPPER AND CARROT SALAD (PAGE 129)

SEARED TILAPIA WITH DRIED FRUIT SPRINKLE

DEHYDRATED APPLES AND ORANGES

2 medium to large apples, peeled, cored and cut into thin rounds

2 navel oranges, peeled, seeded and cut into thin rounds

SEARED TILAPIA

2 pounds boneless tilapia or mackerel fillets, skin on, cut into 5- to 6-ounce pieces

1 ¼ cups cooking oil

1 tablespoon kalonji seeds

3 tablespoons roasted and ground fennel seeds

3 tablespoons ground cumin

1 teaspoon ground cayenne pepper

1 teaspoon salt

If you prefer milder fish, prepare this recipe with tank-farmed tilapia. However, if you love oily, rich-tasting fish, we recommend that you try this recipe with sustainably harvested wild mackerel. Rather than masking the flavour of the tilapia or competing with the rich taste of the mackerel, the combination of rich spices and dried fruit in this dish is a perfect complement to either fish. The result is not the prettiest to look at—but don't be tempted to add anything else or change the colour, or you will upset the balance of flavours.

Preparing the fruit sprinkle takes time, since you have to dry the orange and apple slices in a dehydrator for 10 hours and then grind them. But dehydrating is very simple, once you get used to having a new machine at home. If you don't have a dehydrator or the time to dry the fruit, this dish is delicious without the dried fruit, but the fruit sprinkle really does add an entirely different layering of flavours. Cut the fruit as thinly but as evenly as you can.

At Vij's, we serve the fish over a colourful salad such as the Napa Cabbage in Tomato Masala Salad (page 59) and top it with fried onions and the fruit sprinkle. If you are pressed for time, simply place the seared fish on a big salad that has been tossed with just olive oil, lemon and salt.

SERVES 6

PREP & COOKING TIME: 30 MINUTES + 1 HOUR TO MARINATE + 10 TO 12 HOURS TO DEHYDRATE THE FRUIT (OPTIONAL)

DEHYDRATED APPLES AND ORANGES Arrange the apple and orange slices in a single layer on individual trays in your food dehydrator. Turn on the dehydrator, using the heat setting recommended by the manufacturer for drying fruit. (Our dehydrator took 10 hours to dry the apples and oranges.) Transfer the trays of dehydrated fruit to a wire rack or place them on pot holders on your kitchen counter and allow them to cool to room temperature, about 1 hour.

continued...

Roughly break the fruit, place the pieces in a spice (or coffee) grinder and grind as finely as possible. (There may still be some moistness, and that is okay as long as you don't have chunks of fruit.) Set aside in a small bowl. (Leftover fruit sprinkle will keep in an airtight container at room temperature for 1 week. You can sprinkle leftover fruit on salads or mix it into an oil and vinegar dressing.)

SEARED TILAPIA Place the fish in a large bowl. In a small frying pan, heat ¼ cup of the oil on high heat for 1 minute. Add the kalonji seeds and allow them to sizzle for 20 seconds. Turn off the heat and allow the oil to cool for 5 minutes. Add all of the oil and kalonji to the fish, using a spatula, if necessary.

Add the ground fennel seeds, cumin, cayenne and salt to the fish and mix gently yet thoroughly until the fish is well coated. Cover and refrigerate for 1 hour.

To sear the fish, use a heavy-bottomed frying pan large enough to hold the fillets in one layer and give you enough room to flip them over. (We usually do this in batches, searing 3 fillets at a time in a medium frying pan, using ½ cup of the oil for each of the two batches.) Heat 1 cup of oil (or less, if you are frying in batches) in the pan on high heat for 2 minutes. Reduce the heat to medium-high, place the fish (and all its spices) in the pan and sear on one side for 4 minutes. Gently flip over the fish and sear the other side for 4 minutes. (If you are searing the fish in batches, repeat with the remaining fillets, adding more oil.)

TO SERVE Arrange one fish fillet on each dinner plate. Sprinkle 1 to 1 ½ teaspoons (or more if you enjoy it) of the dried fruit sprinkle on top of each serving. Serve immediately.

SUGGESTED PAIRINGS
NAPA CABBAGE IN TOMATO MASALA SALAD (PAGE 59)
SPICED PICKLE-LIKE CARROTS (PAGE 32)
SPICED SEMOLINA AND ALMOND MASALA ON ORANGE ROUNDS
(PAGE 74)

RAINBOW TROUT IN COCONUT CURRY WITH CURRY LEAVES

In India, fish is very popular (among non-vegetarians), especially white fish that is served lip-burningly hot with a tart finish. The first thing Vikram does whenever he visits his family in Amritsar is to go to his favourite Punjabi fish stand. There the fish is spiced with garam masala and lots of cayenne pepper and finished with lemon. Meeru's father also loves spicy fish, and on a holiday to the old part of Cochin in the southern state of Kerala, he and Meeru stopped at a fish stand. While Meeru sat on a wooden crate balancing the fish on her lap and wiping her spice-induced runny nose, like Vikram her father stood in the street happily enjoying his food. The fish was spiced with ground fenugreek and mustard seeds—and, naturally, lots of cayenne pepper—and finished with a bit of tamarind paste. When Meeru told her father the fish was ridiculously spicy, he fetched her a beer and told her not to speak so disrespectfully about something so quintessentially Indian. Then he sighed as he thought of his vegetarian best friend. "I wish Mahesh-ji would just make special exceptions every once in a while," he said. The Dhalwala and the Vij families are all about making special exceptions when it comes to food!

Fish is a specialty throughout India, but especially in Kerala, where it is prepared in many ways, including with coconut milk and curry leaves. This recipe is inspired by Meeru's trip to Kerala with her father, but instead of the white fish that is common in India, we use rainbow trout. This fish is in the same family as salmon, but it has a milder flavour and less oily texture, and it can soak in a heavier-flavoured curry. As well, most rainbow trout in North America is farmed, so it is often available when salmon is not in season.

In this recipe, we marinate the fish separately, grill it and then pour the curry over it when serving. You may use a bit less oil in the marinade, but remember that oil is crucial to ensure proper grilling and for the spices to cook through while cooking. The star anise is important to the flavour of this curry, so be sure it is fresh and has a strong aroma. At home we sometimes make a more Punjabi version of this curry by leaving out the coconut milk. Serve with plain rice or a rice pilaf.

MARINATED GRILLED TROUT

½ cup cooking oil

3 tablespoons finely chopped garlic (9 to 10 medium cloves)

2 ½ tablespoons ground coriander

2 ½ tablespoons ground cumin

1 ½ tablespoons mild ancho chili powder

1 teaspoon ground cayenne pepper

1 teaspoon salt

3 pounds boneless rainbow trout, skin on, cut into 5- to 6-ounce pieces

continued...

COCONUT CURRY

⅓ cup cooking oil

½ tablespoon black mustard seeds

2 cups finely chopped onions
(1 large)

3 tablespoons chopped garlic
(9 to 10 medium cloves)

12 to 16 fresh curry leaves

4 cups chopped tomatoes
(8 medium)

4 or 5 whole star anise

2 tablespoons ground cumin

1 tablespoon crushed cayenne
pepper

1 tablespoon ground yellow
mustard seeds

1 ½ to 2 teaspoons salt

1 teaspoon turmeric

2 cups premium full-fat coconut
milk, stirred (optional)

4 cups water (if using coconut
milk) or 6 cups water

2 lemons, halved (if not using
coconut milk)

SERVES 8

PREP & COOKING TIME: 1 HOUR + 3 TO 8 HOURS TO MARINATE

MARINATED GRILLED TROUT In a large bowl, combine the oil, garlic, coriander, cumin, ancho chili powder, cayenne and salt. Add the trout, mixing it gently but thoroughly to coat the fish on all sides. Cover and refrigerate for 3 to 8 hours.

COCONUT CURRY WITH CURRY LEAVES Heat the oil in a heavy-bottomed saucepan on medium-high heat for 1 minute. Add the black mustard seeds and heat until they begin to sizzle. As soon as you hear the first few popping sounds, add the onions. Sauté the onions for 8 minutes, or until golden. Stir in the garlic and sauté for 2 minutes, or until golden. Add the curry leaves and cook for 30 seconds, then add the tomatoes, star anise, cumin, cayenne, yellow mustard seeds, salt and turmeric. Cook for 4 to 6 minutes, or until the oil glistens on top.

Stir in the coconut milk and/or water and bring to a boil. Reduce the heat to a simmer, cover and cook for 10 to 15 minutes, or until the oil glistens on top once again. Grill the fish while the curry is simmering.

TO GRILL THE FISH Heat a barbecue or stovetop grill to high until it is nice and hot. Reduce the temperature to medium-high, place the fish skin side down on the grill and cook for 2 ½ to 3 minutes per side. The fish is cooked when it flakes easily when poked gently with a knife. The surface will also become slightly flaky.

TO SERVE Place a piece of grilled fish in the middle of each individual serving bowl. Pour the hot curry around it, until half the fish is submerged in the curry but you can still see the top of it. If you did not use the coconut milk, squeeze some fresh lemon juice over the fish. Serve immediately.

SUGGESTED PAIRINGS
GOLDEN BEET, WHEAT BERRY AND SPROUTED LENTIL SALAD WITH
VIJ'S DRESSING (PAGE 133)
CHICKPEA AND SPROUTED LENTIL CAKES (PAGE 152)
ASSORTED MUSHROOMS AND
WINTER SQUASH CURRY (PAGE 100)

POULTRY

IT'S NOT *MEAT!*

For the three years that we owned our restaurant in Seattle, Meeru travelled there each week. She would leave Vancouver on Wednesday mornings, and Vikram would be with Nanaki and Shanik until late Friday evening, when Meeru would return from Seattle. Meeru would then be with Nanaki and Shanik from Saturday until the next Wednesday morning. We called Friday night our parental "passing of the torch," and we turned it into a fun evening with wine and dinner. Over a late meal, all four of us would catch up on our week. Even if the girls had already eaten, they would still be home to sit with us at the dinner table.

On one of these Fridays, Meeru was returning from ten days in Seattle. Earlier, Vikram had asked her what she wanted for dinner. She had responded that she'd been eating way too much meat, and she requested a vegetarian meal. When Meeru got home, a bottle of red wine was open and the dinner table was set. After saying our hellos, we all sat down to eat. Vikram had made oven-roasted chicken with French green lentil curry.

We all have these moments when someone has worked hard to please you but didn't listen to what you wanted. At times like these, no matter how well you know someone, it's a difficult decision: do you act very happy and thankful (which you actually are, but not entirely) or do you risk coming across as whiny or ungrateful and point out that you had asked for a vegetarian dinner and got chicken instead. Meeru asked Vikram why, if he was going to ask her what she wanted for dinner and say yes, no problem, to vegetarian food, he had served chicken. His answer: "You said no meat, so I made you chicken. And look at all these lentils that will fill all your vegetarian nooks and crannies!"

Vikram pretty much thinks that chicken is in its own food category but obviously not meat. He's not alone. A few of our kitchen staff who have been vegetarian their whole lives have started eating chicken. It's like a gateway meat for them. We asked one of them why she has begun to eat chicken, and she said, "We get the protein and the iron but we don't feel that we're eating meat with the red blood." Similarly, a couple came in for dinner on a Friday night; the woman explained that she was vegetarian but her husband was not. After their server had explained the menu, the husband ordered the lamb popsicles and she ordered the chicken curry. They were served their dinner, both enjoyed themselves, and they asked to have their leftovers packed up for them. The next morning, we received a very angry email from the woman stating that we had totally disrespected her choices because her husband's lamb sauce had been mixed in with her chicken. Our staff was dumbfounded until Meeru explained that, while it's a stretch to call yourself vegetarian and order chicken curry, many people don't consider chicken the same as red meat. In their minds, chicken is in a class of its own—probably because chicken breast is a white meat.

Whether you call yourself a vegetarian, pollo-vegetarian, meat eater or something entirely different, if you eat chicken, choose wisely. A lot of the chicken sold in supermarkets is "cheap": the birds have been raised in crowded, dirty conditions and treated with antibiotics to prevent the spread of disease. In our minds, this is the worst type of food for your body, the environment and the animal. The terms "free run" and "cage free" mean only that the chickens are not always in cages, not that the other conditions are any different. At home and for our restaurants, we buy organic chicken or chickens "raised without the use of antibiotics." This is still less expensive than organic or natural red meat or sustainable seafood. We also share the belief that the soup stock made from chicken bones is good for colds and flus. So for taste and health, we urge you to buy all-natural or organic chicken. We prefer to cook with bone-in thighs, drumsticks and wings—not just the breasts. As for the weight of chicken, we give estimates in the recipes but it's okay to buy, say, half a pound more than what we've written, as fat and bones are included in the given weight.

OVEN-BAKED CHICKEN WITH CHARD
AND RED RADISHES

2 pounds chicken wings or
bone-in thighs

¼ cup cooking oil

2 tablespoons chopped garlic
(6 to 7 medium cloves)

1 ½ tablespoons mild ancho chili
powder

1 ½ tablespoons ground cumin

2 teaspoons salt

½ tablespoon dried oregano

6 whole cloves

2 cups puréed fresh or canned
tomatoes (5 to 6 medium)

2 bunches chard (any kind), stems
discarded, chopped

1 bunch red radishes

1 small head cauliflower, cut into
large pieces, OR 1 pound potatoes,
chopped into large pieces, OR
1 pound fresh green beans,
chopped

1 lemon, cut into 6 wedges
(optional)

SUGGESTED PAIRINGS
NAVY BEANS IN EGG AND TOMATO
MASALA (PAGE 158)
MILLET AND BELL PEPPER PILAF
(PAGE 144)

This no-nonsense curry-flavoured dish is our first-ever Indian meal made with chard … and oregano. We make this easy meal at home all the time, and it's a favourite of Nanaki and Shanik's friends when they join us for dinner.

The red radishes are a must: they become sweet when cooked, and much of their colour goes into the curry itself. If the leaves of the radishes are in good shape, wash them and include them in the curry too. And though we suggest cauliflower, potatoes, green beans (or a combination of them), we add any vegetables we're in the mood for that fit into the casserole dish. When you mix the vegetables into the tomatoes, it will look like you have way too many, but remember that chard wilts as it cooks.

We cook with bone-in chicken, either wings or thighs. When we're in the mood for full fat and rich flavour, we cook with the wings. When we want extra chicken, we use the thighs. To get the fatty flavour without getting all the fat, we take the skin off half of the thighs and leave the skin on the other half. We serve this chicken with a baguette or rice pilaf.

SERVES 6

PREP & COOKING TIME: 45 MINUTES

PREHEAT the oven to 400°F. Have ready a 9- × 12-inch casserole dish and a sheet of aluminum foil large enough to cover it.

Place the chicken pieces in a large bowl. Add the oil, garlic, ancho chili powder, cumin, 1 teaspoon of the salt, the oregano and cloves. Using your hands, mix well until the chicken is well coated.

Pour the tomatoes into the casserole dish. The next step is messy, so place the casserole dish on the counter or somewhere that's easy to clean up. Add the chard, radishes, cauliflower (or potatoes or green beans) and salt and mix until the vegetables are well combined with the tomatoes. Once the vegetables are mixed, use your hands to press down on the vegetables so you have room to add the chicken.

Arrange the chicken on top of the vegetables (be sure to scrape all the garlic and oil from the mixing bowl), cover loosely with the aluminum foil and bake for 30 minutes. Remove from the oven, carefully pull back the foil (there will be lots of hot steam) and take a peek. If you are cooking chicken wings, they will be done. If you're baking thighs, poke the tip of a knife into the thickest part of a thigh to check that the middle is thoroughly cooked—it will be juicy but there will be no pink meat in the centre.

TO SERVE Serve family style right from the casserole dish, piping hot and with a pair of large serving spoons so everyone can help themselves. Serve with lemon wedges on the side, if you like.

CHICKEN AND LOCAL VEGETABLE CURRY

½ cup cooking oil

3 tablespoons finely chopped garlic (9 to 10 medium cloves)

12 ounces fresh tomatoes (4 to 5 medium), roughly chopped

1 ½ tablespoons ground cumin

½ tablespoon salt

1 teaspoon turmeric

1 teaspoon ground cayenne pepper

1 teaspoon ground fenugreek seeds

12 ounces turnip, peeled and chopped into 1-inch squares

12 ounces green beans, chopped into ¾- to 1-inch pieces

4 ounces green leaves, such as kale or mustard, stems discarded if need be, chopped

½ tablespoon dried green fenugreek leaves

12 ounces to 1 pound skinless, boneless chicken thighs, cut into 2-inch pieces

This recipe, including the chicken, is designed to "decorate" any seasonal vegetable in a simple and delicious way. We enjoy turnips, but you can easily substitute carrots, golden beets or potatoes for the turnips, or fresh green peas for the green beans. Aim for a mix of different vegetables and colours. Since we encourage you to use whichever vegetables are grown where you live and to adjust the ratio of chicken to vegetables according to your personal preference, your cooking times may be different from the ones we've suggested below. The chicken, however, takes 10 to 12 minutes to cook.

Note that there is lots of garlic relative to the other ingredients in this curry: it suits the ingredients no matter which vegetables you choose—as long as you use the same overall quantities. Unless you are not a big fan of garlic, be bold with it. We enjoy the depth of the fenugreek on fenugreek, since the seeds and the leaves have such different flavours. The fenugreek seed is crucial to the recipe, but if you don't have the dried green fenugreek leaves, you can substitute chopped cilantro. Pay close attention when you're measuring out these two ingredients, because if you use even slightly too much of the ground seeds, they won't match well with the green leaves; this is why we don't often combine the two fenugreeks in a single recipe.

At Vij's, we serve this dish with the Sweet and Savoury Millet Pilaf with Fennel Seeds (page 143), but it is delicious with any rice pilaf.

SERVES 6 TO 8

PREP & COOKING TIME: 45 MINUTES

HEAT ¼ CUP of the oil in a medium-large pot on medium-high heat for 1 minute. Add the garlic and sauté for 2 minutes, or until golden. Stir in the tomatoes, then add the cumin, salt, turmeric, cayenne and fenugreek seeds. Sauté, stirring frequently, for 4 to 5 minutes, or until the oil glistens on top of the masala. Reduce the heat to medium, add the turnips, stir and cover. After 4 minutes, add the green beans, stir and continue cooking, uncovered, for 3 to 4 minutes. Stir in the greens and cook for 2 minutes. Add the fenugreek leaves and turn off the heat.

In a medium, heavy-bottomed frying pan, heat the remaining ¼ cup of oil on high heat for 1 minute. Add the chicken and cook, stirring gently, for 3 minutes, or until slightly browned. Reduce the heat to medium-low, cover and cook for another 7 minutes. Remove the lid and gently poke a thigh with the tip of a knife to ensure that it is cooked completely—there should be no pink in the centre. If it is not quite done, cover and cook for another 2 to 3 minutes—but be careful not to overcook the chicken. Stir the chicken and all of its juices into the pot of vegetables.

TO SERVE Heat the chicken and vegetables, uncovered, on medium-high heat for 2 to 4 minutes, stirring regularly. Transfer the chicken curry to a large casserole dish and serve family style.

SUGGESTED PAIRINGS
SWEET AND SAVOURY MILLET PILAF WITH FENNEL SEEDS (PAGE 143)
**LAMB SHANK AND GREENS CURRY WITH
"ETHIOPIAN FLAG" BASMATI RICE PILAF (PAGE 221)**
BENGALI-STYLE BLACK BEAN AND CORN CURRY (PAGE 162)

SIMPLE GRILLED CHICKEN WITH OPTIONAL SPICE SPRINKLE

1 tablespoon cumin seeds

½ tablespoon coriander seeds

½ teaspoon ajwain seeds

1 teaspoon mango powder (break up any clumps)

1 teaspoon ground dried mint (optional)

2 ½ pounds skinless, boneless chicken thighs (or 3 pounds bone-in)

½ cup canola or grapeseed oil

1 tablespoon salt

1 tablespoon mild ancho chili powder

1 teaspoon ground cayenne pepper

When made with boneless thighs and served on buns with Sour Cream Dressing (page 27), this recipe makes great chicken burgers. Most often, though, we serve this simple grilled chicken alongside vegetarian dishes. It's a simpler version of the marinated and grilled chicken we serve at Rangoli.

In the summer of 2015 Nanaki worked full-time as a server at Rangoli. Vikram and Meeru laughed to think that our one child who has a limited (but sincere) capacity for Indian food would be surrounded by Indian food and eating it every day for her staff meal. When Vikram asked her after a few weeks if she was getting sick of Indian food, she replied, "No—there's always the grilled chicken." (Meeru, in turn, began to wonder if Nanaki was eating too much meat.)

The chicken will need a few hours to marinate before you cook it. If you really want to keep things simple, with no heat, you can forgo the cayenne pepper. If you choose to make the optional spice sprinkle, roast and grind your spices while the chicken is marinating. (You can easily double the spice recipe and reserve some for another time.) Prepare your condiments and side dishes at that time too. Bone-in chicken will be just that much juicier, and we recommend that you keep it on the bone when serving. Unless you're making chicken burgers.

SERVES 6
PREP & COOKING TIME: 35 TO 40 MINUTES
+ 3 TO 8 HOURS TO MARINATE

SUGGESTED PAIRINGS
ZUCCHINI, SQUASH AND POTATO SAUTÉ (PAGE 106)
BENGALI-STYLE CURRY (PAGE 36)
SPROUTED LENTIL, BELL PEPPER AND CARROT SALAD (PAGE 129)

HEAT a small, heavy-bottomed frying pan on high heat for 1 minute. Add the cumin, coriander and ajwain seeds and roast the seeds, stirring constantly, for 1 to 2 minutes, or until the cumin and coriander darken and give off a strong aroma. Transfer the seeds to a bowl and allow them to cool for 15 minutes. Grind them in a spice (or coffee) grinder.

Pour the ground roasted spices into a small bowl, add the mango powder and mint and mix well. Set aside or transfer to an airtight container and store in a dark cupboard or drawer for up to 3 months (the mango powder loses its aroma after that time).

In a large bowl, mix the chicken with the oil, salt, chili powder and cayenne until well combined. Cover and refrigerate for 3 to 8 hours. The longer the marinating time, the stronger the flavour of the ancho chili.

Heat a barbecue or a stovetop grill on high. Place the chicken on the grill and cook for 4 to 5 minutes per side, or until it is cooked through. (Poke a thigh with the tip of a knife after 4 minutes. If there is no pink inside, then it is cooked.) Be careful not to overcook the chicken.

Transfer the hot chicken to a serving platter and sprinkle it, as you would salt, with the ground spice mixture.

TO SERVE Place the serving platter in the middle of the table, family style.

MILD TURMERIC AND GHEE CHICKEN CURRY

⅓ cup ghee

3 pounds skinless, bone-in chicken thighs

1 cup finely chopped onions (1 medium-large)

2 cups chopped tomatoes (5 to 6 medium)

1 tablespoon chopped ginger (optional)

2 teaspoons salt

2 teaspoons mild ancho chili powder (optional)

½ tablespoon turmeric

½ cup plain yogurt (minimum 2% milk fat), stirred

7 cups water

½ cup chopped cilantro (optional)

1 bunch green onions, finely chopped (optional)

3 cups cooked rice (preferably Basmati), hot

Whether or not you prefer mild curries, you will love this dish. Served with plain white rice and some mango or lemon pickle on the side, this chicken curry is the perfect generational family comfort curry, and it's as delicious as any spicy version. If you are serving this dish to kids for the first time, the cilantro and green onions are optional. Even if you don't add them to the curry itself, we suggest you chop these ingredients finely, place them in small bowls and serve them at the table so diners can add their own.

When Meeru was growing up, chicken curry was a cherished weekend treat in her family. Her mom made it mild and soupy, just the way Meeru and her sister, Ritu, loved it, but she always insisted on adding tons of tiny pieces of ginger—which the girls didn't enjoy. This spice (and turmeric), she believed, was the key to proper digestion, especially of meats and legumes. In our own family, we still add the ginger, but we cut it into bigger, more visible pieces so that Nanaki and Shanik can take it out according to their preferences and Vikram and Meeru can still enjoy lots of ginger.

We prefer the caramelized flavour of ghee in this dish, and in India it's common to pair ghee and yogurt, especially with less spicy curries. You can use butter instead of ghee if you like, but remember to sauté the masala over lower heat, because butter burns. As well, be sure to use a yogurt with some fat in it (we use full-fat plain yogurt) for a full flavour.

We serve the chicken bone-in at the table, as it is easy to remove the tender meat from the bones with a spoon or fork. If you prefer, you can allow the curry to cool, take the meat off the bones and return the meat to the curry. Reheat the curry over medium-high heat just until it begins to boil, about 10 minutes, before serving.

SERVES 6

PREP & COOKING TIME: 1 HOUR

IN A LARGE pot, melt the ghee on medium-high heat. Add the chicken and sauté for 5 minutes, or until lightly browned. Stir in the onions and sauté for 5 minutes, stirring regularly, until they are light golden. Add the tomatoes, ginger, salt, ancho chili powder and turmeric and stir well. Sauté for 8 to 10 minutes, or until all the liquid from the tomatoes has evaporated. Reduce the heat to low.

Place the yogurt in a small bowl. Stir a dollop of the tomato masala into the yogurt. (This step prevents the yogurt from splitting once it hits the hot masala.) Stir the yogurt into the tomato masala and cook for 5 minutes, or until the mixture is well combined. Pour in the water and stir well, then increase the heat to medium-high and bring to a boil. Reduce the heat to low, cover and simmer for 15 minutes, or until the chicken is cooked and the oil from the ghee glistens on top of the curry.

If all of your guests are okay with cilantro and green onions, stir them into the chicken curry once it is cooked. If not, serve them separately in small bowls so those who like them can help themselves.

TO SERVE Divide the rice evenly among 6 large individual bowls. Ladle about ¾ cup of the chicken curry over each portion of rice.

SUGGESTED PAIRINGS
BITTER GOURD WITH POTATOES AND ONIONS (PAGE 116)
COCONUT JAPANESE-INDIAN GREEN BEAN CURRY (PAGE 98)
CREAMY FENUGREEK AND CUMIN POTATOES (PAGE 96)

GREEN AND BLACK CARDAMOM CREAM CHICKEN CURRY

CARDAMOM CURRY

1 cup water

½ to ¾ teaspoon green cardamom seeds (6 to 8 whole green cardamom pods)

½ teaspoon black cardamom seeds (3 to 4 whole black cardamom pods)

⅓ cup cooking oil

1 tablespoon cumin seeds

3 tablespoons chopped ginger

1 to 2 tablespoons chopped jalapeño pepper (depends on the heat of each pepper)

1 cup canned crushed tomatoes OR 2 cups puréed very, very ripe tomatoes (5 to 6 medium)

1 teaspoon salt

1 teaspoon turmeric

1 teaspoon ground fenugreek seeds

4 cups whipping cream

SAUTÉED CHICKEN

⅓ cup cooking oil

3 ½ pounds skinless, bone-in chicken thighs

2 cups water

1 teaspoon salt

At Vij's, we call this our creamy chai curry because it is cardamom based. Even though it does not deliver the predictable onion-garlic "curry" taste that people associate with Indian food, this delicious curry *is* all Indian, and it's a delightful change from the usual flavours.

As you make this recipe, it's important to keep in mind two things. First, use the quantities set out here and do not delete any ingredients—otherwise the recipe will come out tasting flat. Second, be sure that you use cardamoms with a strong fresh aroma, otherwise you'll get a flavourless curry. Do not be surprised if you have to discard some of the cardamom pods in the package you purchase. We do this every day at our restaurants and at home when making chai. With the side of a knife, lightly crack the cardamom pods. With your fingers, peel back the shells to release the seeds and collect them in a small bowl. The best seeds are dark and stuck together, so keep peeling away until you find the fresh seeds with the strong aroma. Discard the shells.

You can serve the cardamom cream curry with any roasted or sautéed vegetables, but here we've provided a simple bone-in chicken recipe. Use any cut of chicken, including boneless if you want to skip the step of taking the cooked chicken off the bone before adding it to the curry.

SERVES 6
PREP & COOKING TIME: **1 HOUR**

CARDAMOM CURRY In a very small pot, bring the water and the green and black cardamom seeds to a boil on high heat. Reduce the heat to low, allow the seeds to simmer for 5 minutes, then turn off the heat, cover and allow to steep for 30 minutes to 1 hour. If you don't mind having the seeds in your curry, leave them in the water and set aside. If you'd rather not, strain the mixture through a fine-mesh sieve into a clean bowl. Discard the seeds and reserve the water.

Heat the oil in a large frying pan on medium-high heat for 1 minute. Add the cumin seeds and allow them to sizzle for 15 seconds. Stir in the ginger and sauté for up to 1 minute. Add the jalapeños and sauté for another minute, stirring well. Reduce the heat to medium and stir in the tomatoes. Add the salt, turmeric and fenugreek. Stir and sauté for 3 minutes, or until the oil glistens on top of the tomato masala. Turn off the heat.

SAUTÉED CHICKEN Heat the oil in a frying pan on medium-high heat. Add the chicken and sauté, turning occasionally, until lightly browned, about 10 minutes. Pour in the water and salt, stir well, then cover and reduce the heat to medium. Cook the chicken for 15 to 20 minutes, or until it is cooked through. (Poke the chicken with the tip of a knife—there should be no pink in the centre.) Turn off the heat and transfer the chicken to a large bowl to cool for about 20 minutes. Reserve the cooking water (stock).

Once the chicken is cooled, take the meat off the bones. Discard the bones. Combine the chicken meat with the stock. Set aside.

FINISH CURRY In a medium bowl, combine the cardamom water with the whipping cream. Add the mixture to the tomato masala, stirring well to combine, and bring to a boil on medium-high heat. Add the chicken and its stock. Reduce the heat to a simmer, cover and warm through for 5 minutes.

TO SERVE Transfer the chicken curry to a large casserole dish and serve family style—or ladle into individual bowls.

SUGGESTED PAIRINGS
QUINOA AND CAULIFLOWER SALAD (PAGE 130)
SWEET AND SAVOURY MILLET PILAF WITH FENNEL SEEDS (PAGE 143)
CAULIFLOWER AND POTATO IN TOMATO MASALA (PAGE 111)

INDIAN-JAPANESE CHICKEN-VEGETABLE
SOBA NOODLE CURRY

ORGANIC CHICKEN STOCK

5 to 6 organic chicken necks and backs

7 cups water

4 stalks celery, roughly chopped

½ to 1 tablespoon roughly chopped ginger

1 teaspoon ground black pepper

VEGETABLE CURRY

⅓ cup cooking oil

1 cup finely chopped red onions (1 medium)

2 tablespoons finely chopped garlic (6 to 7 medium cloves)

1 tablespoon ground cumin

1 teaspoon turmeric

1 teaspoon crushed cayenne pepper

1 teaspoon salt

1 cup chopped fresh tomatoes (2 to 3 medium)

½ pound brown mushrooms, thinly sliced

½ pound carrots, thinly sliced (optional)

1 bunch green onions, white and green parts, finely chopped

1 box (16 ounces) dry soba, udon or ramen noodles

½ cup finely chopped cilantro, stems included

Japanese tamari or shoyu soy sauce to taste

This light and healthy Japanese-Indian curry noodle soup was one of the most popular dishes of all time among our staff at Rangoli. For the year that we had this recipe on our menu, Akiko Masutani, who was our front-of-house manager at the time (she is now at Vij's), ate it at least three days a week. Our kitchen staff loved this recipe too. Although we stopped serving this curry soup at the restaurant years ago, we still eat it often at home and serve it at dinner parties. It's a comforting dish that combines everything we love about Japanese and Indian food. Heavy spicing doesn't work with the delicate Japanese flavours.

If you are pressed for time, you can buy about 6 cups of chicken or vegetable stock and perhaps use less soy sauce, since store-bought stocks are high in sodium. But for the ideal curry, we highly recommend that you make the organic chicken stock in this recipe. (To save time, you can prepare the masala while the stock is cooking.) We use soba (buckwheat) noodles for their health benefits, but you can substitute udon or ramen if you prefer. Prepare the noodles last and be careful not to overcook them.

Serve Japanese soy sauce at the table and let everyone decide for themselves how much they wish to use. Tamari is the deeper-coloured and stronger-tasting soy sauce, while shoyu is the all-purpose and lighter tasting of the two. (Note that lighter tasting doesn't mean less sodium.)

SERVES 6
PREP & COOKING TIME: 1 ½ HOURS (IF MAKING THE STOCK) OR 45 MINUTES (IF USING STORE-BOUGHT STOCK)

ORGANIC CHICKEN STOCK Rinse the chicken necks and backs under cold running water and place them in a large stockpot. Add the water, celery, ginger and black pepper; bring to a boil on high heat. Reduce the heat to a simmer, and use a small fine-mesh sieve to gently skim off and discard the foam that collects on the surface for the first 15 minutes or so. Once the water is clear and gently boiling, simmer, covered, for 45 minutes.

Place a fine-mesh sieve over a large clean pot. Carefully pour the stock through the sieve. Set aside the solids and allow them to cool.

There will be small and quite delicious morsels of chicken meat on the bones. If you want to add these pieces to your stock, it will take no more than 10 minutes or so to get them off the bone and add them to the broth. Discard or compost the bones and vegetable pieces. Otherwise, just compost all the solids—chicken meat, bones and vegetables. Set the stock aside.

VEGETABLE CURRY Heat the oil in a medium pot on medium-high heat for 1 minute. Add the onions and sauté for 8 minutes, or until golden. Stir in the garlic and sauté for another 2 minutes. Add the cumin, turmeric, cayenne and salt and sauté for 2 minutes. Stir in the tomatoes, mushrooms, carrots and green onions, mixing well, and cook for 2 minutes more. Transfer the vegetable mixture to the pot with the chicken stock, and stir well to combine.

Bring a large pot of water to a boil on high heat. Add the noodles and cook according to the instructions on the package. Immediately drain the noodles in a colander and run cold water over them to stop the cooking.

TO SERVE Bring the vegetable curry to a boil on high heat. Immediately reduce the heat to low and simmer for 2 to 3 minutes. Divide the cooked noodles among individual bowls, then pour equal portions of the vegetable curry over the noodles. Garnish with cilantro and soy sauce. Serve immediately.

SUGGESTED PAIRINGS
NAVY BEANS IN EGG AND TOMATO MASALA (PAGE 158)
SAUTÉED BRUSSELS SPROUTS SALAD (PAGE 90)
COCONUT JAPANESE-INDIAN GREEN BEAN CURRY,
FOR A FULL INDIAN-JAPANESE MEAL (PAGE 98)

CLAY POT SAFFRON CHICKEN AND RICE

½ teaspoon dark red saffron threads

¼ cup hot water

⅓ cup cooking oil

1 tablespoon cumin seeds

2 cups chopped onions (1 large)

¼ teaspoon asafoetida

1 tablespoon ground coriander

1 teaspoon turmeric

1 teaspoon salt

½ teaspoon ground cayenne pepper

5 cups water

2 cups Basmati rice

3 pounds skinless, bone-in chicken thighs (or 2 pounds boneless)

This richly flavoured recipe is similar to one that Vikram learned in Hyderabad during an informal cooking demo from one of the cooks at the hotel where he was staying. This Indian city is well known for its meat biryanis, which are often slow-cooked. Vikram is a big fan of slow-cooking chicken and red meats in clay pots because this method results in very tender and succulent meats. At My Shanti, we make individual servings of this dish in small clay pots. Here we've simplified the preparation by providing instructions for a single large clay pot or a Dutch oven.

This dish is fairly easy to prepare, elegant in its presentation and, though mildly spiced, very flavourful. For best results, be sure to use high-quality dark red threads of saffron—otherwise you will not get much flavour, no matter how much you use. Bone-in chicken will give the rice a deeper flavour, but because there is no broth you can also use boneless chicken here. Serve 5 to 6 ounces of chicken meat per person. When we prepare this recipe at home, we often sprinkle 1 cup of salted Sprouted Lentils (page 42) on top before serving.

SERVES 6

PREP & COOKING TIME: 1 HOUR

IN A SMALL bowl, soak the saffron threads in the ¼ cup of hot water for 20 to 30 minutes. Set aside.

Preheat the oven to 375°F. Have ready a 4- to 5-quart Dutch oven or clay pot.

Heat the oil in a medium-large pot on medium-high heat for 1 minute. Add the cumin seeds and allow them to sizzle for 15 seconds. Stir in the onions and sauté for 8 minutes, or until golden. Add the asafoetida and sauté for 1 minute. Stir in the coriander, turmeric, salt and cayenne; sauté for 3 minutes. Pour in the 5 cups of water, stir to combine and turn off the heat. Stir in the saffron and its soaking water. Set aside.

Place the rice in a medium bowl, wash it well under cold water and drain. Repeat the washing and draining once more. Spread the

continued...

rice evenly in the Dutch oven. Arrange the chicken thighs in a single layer on top of the rice, then pour the onion-saffron curry over the chicken. Cover and bake for 40 minutes.

Remove the pot from the oven and carefully remove the lid (hot steam will be escaping). With the tip of a sharp knife, poke a piece of chicken to ensure that it is cooked thoroughly. If it is still pink in the centre, cover and return to the oven for another 5 minutes.

TO SERVE Bring the Dutch oven to the table and serve family style.

SUGGESTED PAIRINGS
PLAIN SPROUTED LENTILS (PAGE 42) OR SPROUTED LENTIL,
BELL PEPPER AND CARROT SALAD (PAGE 129)
YAMS, MUSHROOMS, GREEN BEANS AND ASPARAGUS IN
CUMIN AND FENUGREEK CURRY (PAGE 102)
LENTIL CURRY WITH SAUTÉED EGGPLANT, POTATOES AND
FENNEL (PAGE 156)

DUCK BREAST AND FRESH MANGOES

Like most Indians, we love mangoes and we use them a lot in our home recipes and at the restaurants. When Vikram was growing up in Mumbai, he and his family eagerly awaited Alphonso mango season (from mid-April to June). The arrival of ripe Alphonso mangoes from the middle Indian states of Gujarat and Maharashtra is a big deal in Mumbai, as these mangoes are considered to be among the most superior in aroma (with hints of rose), texture (fleshy and much less fibrous) and taste. Each day during mango season, Vikram's father would make a trip to the market after work to buy a box of a dozen mangoes that the family would eat for dessert and in milkshakes the next morning. Vikram would get in trouble for eating too many of these mangoes. (It's a common Indian belief that eating too many mangoes gives you major acne.)

Alphonso mangoes are difficult to get in North America because they do not pack well for travel. In Vancouver, we mostly get Ataulfo, Kent or Tommy Atkins mangoes from Mexico or South America. Mangoes are actually the most eaten fruit in the world. No matter the type of mango, for us eating one is like remembering India in the fondest way. We do not limit ourselves to eating them on their own, however. Sweet mango chutneys have long accompanied many entrées, but fresh mango can hold up to many savoury food partners. Our latest favourite pairing is with rich, gamey duck breast.

This particular recipe can be made in many ways. The simplest—as here—is to sear the duck on your stovetop and serve it with mangoes. The most ornate and layered way is to serve the seared duck breast and mango with Indian vegetarian toppings. For example, if you've taken the plunge and prepared the Bitter Gourd with Potatoes and Onions (page 116), adding duck breast and mango makes for a very different and stunning Indian dish. You can also serve duck breast and fresh mangoes on top of any rice or millet pilaf. Or, easier, serve this dish with the coconut curry base from the Eggplant, Kale and Cauliflower Curry (page 88); do not add the eggplant, kale or cauliflower.

SERVES 6 TO 8

PREP & COOKING TIME: 45 MINUTES

3 fresh, ripe mangoes, peeled, pitted and cut into 1-inch chunks

½ cup chopped cilantro, stems included

½ tablespoon finely chopped ginger (optional)

½ teaspoon freshly ground black pepper (optional)

2 teaspoons salt

6 skin-on, boneless duck breasts

continued...

IN A LARGE bowl, combine the mangoes, cilantro, ginger, black pepper and ½ teaspoon of the salt. Set aside or refrigerate, covered, if you will not be serving for a while.

Using your hands, rub the remaining 1 ½ teaspoons of salt over the duck breasts, making sure to cover both sides. With a paring knife, score the skin of each breast in two diagonal lines about ¼ inch deep. (Be careful not to cut into the duck meat.) This step helps the fat to render while you are searing the duck breasts.

Line a large plate with paper towels. Heat a large, heavy frying pan on medium heat for 3 to 4 minutes. Arrange as many breasts, skin side down, as will fit in the pan. The breasts will most likely make a loud sizzling noise immediately—do not be alarmed. Cook on one side for 8 to 10 minutes, or until the fat has rendered and the skin looks crispy and golden. Turn the breasts over and cook for 3 minutes. This gives you a distinctive reddish-pink centre in the breast. If you wish to cook the meat more, sear the breast for an additional 2 minutes on the second side. Transfer the duck to the paper towel–lined plate. Repeat with any remaining duck breasts. Discard the duck fat, or better yet, pour it through a fine-mesh sieve and reserve the fat for future cooking.

TO SERVE Using a sharp knife, cut the duck breasts into ⅓-inch slices. You want to serve the equivalent of one duck breast per person, about 6 ounces each. Arrange an equal number of slices on each plate and top with the mangoes. Serve immediately.

SUGGESTED PAIRINGS

BITTER GOURD WITH POTATOES AND ONIONS—PLACE THE DUCK AND MANGOES ON TOP (PAGE 116)

EGGPLANT, KALE AND CAULIFLOWER CURRY—THE CURRY SAUCE ONLY (PAGE 88)

ZUCCHINI, SQUASH AND POTATO SAUTÉ (PAGE 106)

MEATS

BONE-IN MEATS

We do our best to be a meat-once-a-week family. This is easy for Shanik and Meeru, but Vikram and Nanaki (except when she's cooking for herself at university) have to make an effort to eat less meat. Even Vikram, who loves his meats, believes strongly that eating meat more than once or twice a week isn't a healthy choice for the body or the environment. Shanik's favourite dinner table guilt story is about the Amazon rain forest being clear-cut to raise cows, which eat vegetarian food that starving people could otherwise eat. If Vikram doesn't tell her to be quiet at this point—before Nanaki yells at her sister to shut up—Shanik will go on to the carbon footprint of raising cows. For Vikram especially, the temptation to enjoy beef, pork or lamb stews, roasts and curries will sometimes test his resolve and common sense about health.

A meat-once-a-week diet makes it more affordable to buy organic and sustainably raised meats. Nanaki has no problem eating such meats. Shanik still needs a little more convincing. However, none of us wants to follow any diet that restricts our enjoyment of foods. We believe that our Indian bodies are adapted to the foods our ancestors have been eating for generations. Chapatti (whole-wheat and bran flatbread) is our staple, so there's little chance of a gluten-free diet. And yogurt is our source of all good bacteria, so there goes the vegan and lactose-free diets. Similarly, we've been a vegetarian population for thousands of years. A meat-heavy diet would probably kill us prematurely! We do believe, though, that cooking with animal bones provides our bodies with the enzymes to digest the meat properly. A boneless beef short rib or tenderloin is delicious, but we imagine our bodies asking what to do with that protein and fat once it passes our taste buds. Our Indian parents also taught us that all lives, including animal lives, matter and that eating the meat of an improperly treated animal brings bad energy to our bodies. So, choose the best-quality meat you can afford, remembering that quality isn't just the taste of the meat but also how the animal was raised and what it ate.

In our Indian eating traditions, all soupy-style meat curries (which are always goat, chicken or lamb, in accordance with the Hindu and Muslim religions) are made with the bones, and the bone-in stock is as valued as the meat itself. However, eating a bone-in curry in North America can sometimes be an uncomfortable experience. Indians don't use

dinner knives or forks. The spoon and our hands are an integral part of our traditional dining culture. And using your hands to pick the meat from the bones in a soupy curry at the dinner table is considered messy business. What do you do with all the curry on your hands? For one thing, you rest both elbows on the table. Our fathers and their friends enjoy slurping every bit of meat and marrow from the bones, and they just lick their fingers (and sometimes the side of their hand to catch any curry before it drips down their arm). If Vikram is eating with one of the fathers, he too will lick his curried fingers and suck on bones and marrow. Meeru is more comfortable eating with a spoon, even though she can't get every last bit of marrow and meat from the bone.

Cultural eating habits are a subject we've given much thought to. We don't want to waste food or lose the enjoyment of savouring our food deeply or sharing it with our friends, but we realize that the visual ambiance is an important part of a meal too. And if you're not born into a culture that slurps marrow and licks its hands, it's not a pretty sight and it's not easy to feel comfortable doing it. For this reason, we make the effort to cook our meat curries bone-in, allow them to cool just enough to handle the meat, and then don rubber gloves and take the meat off the bones before mixing it back into the curry to serve at the table. It means a more comfortable meal for our guests—at the restaurants and at home—who don't want to get their hands dirty. (It also saves us from having to deal with extremely dirty dinner napkins!)

However often you eat meat and however you choose to eat it—with your hands or with a knife and fork—do try the bone-in recipes. Made with good-quality meats, they're full of flavour, full of healthy minerals and a good way to stretch your grocery dollars.

BEEF SHORT RIBS IN KALONJI AND CREAM CURRY

⅓ cup cooking oil

1 tablespoon kalonji seeds

1 tablespoon finely chopped or ground ginger

20 to 25 fresh curry leaves (optional)

1 cup crushed tomatoes

2 tablespoons mild ancho chili powder

2 tablespoons ground coriander

1 tablespoon ground black mustard seeds

1 teaspoon ground fenugreek seeds

1 tablespoon salt

½ to 1 teaspoon ground cayenne pepper

4 cups cold water

3 cups whipping cream OR 2 cups premium full-fat coconut milk, stirred

4 to 4 ½ pounds bone-in beef short ribs, cut into 11- to 12-ounce pieces along the bone and trimmed of extra fat

We developed this recipe in response to a request from a regular customer who is allergic to onions and garlic, because we had no dishes at the time that didn't contain these two core Indian ingredients. This dish has now become by far our most popular beef short rib dish ever at Rangoli, and what astonishes our customers is how few spices we use to achieve such rich and complex flavour. The flavour of the bones in the stock becomes one of the "spices." We prefer to use bone-in short ribs for this reason and for their added nutritional value, but you can use boneless meat if you prefer. One serving of beef short rib is 6 to 7 ounces of meat. (You will lose some of the original weight of the meat because much of the fat will cook into the curry; it is easy to skim off at the end.) You can ask your butcher to chop the short ribs. Don't be afraid of the salt, as the dish needs it to balance the cream. And if you can find fragrant fresh green curry leaves, they'll add a distinct, slightly "curry" taste to this dish. If they are not fresh, however, they won't impart any flavour at all. Serve this dish as we do at the restaurant, with pickled vegetables, rice and naan (or bread).

SERVES 6
PREP & COOKING TIME: 1 ½ TO 2 HOURS, MOSTLY COOKING TIME

IN A LARGE stockpot, heat the oil on medium-high heat for 1 minute. Add the kalonji seeds and allow them to sizzle for 45 seconds. Reduce the heat to medium and, keeping your face away from the pot, stir in the ginger, curry leaves and tomatoes (these may splatter once they hit the hot oil). Immediately add the ancho chili powder, coriander, mustard seeds, fenugreek, salt and cayenne. Cook for 2 to 3 minutes, or until the oil glistens on top.

Pour in the water and then add the whipping cream (or coconut milk), stirring until well combined. (It's important to add the water first, as it prevents the whipping cream from splitting when it is mixed into the hot masala. Coconut milk will not separate.) Add the beef short ribs and stir well. Increase the heat to high

continued...

and bring the mixture to a boil, then reduce the heat to low, cover and cook for 1 ½ to 2 hours, stirring occasionally. The meat is cooked when it is tender and easily falls from the bone when poked with the tip of a knife. Turn off the heat.

Using a ladle or a large spoon, skim off and discard the fat on the surface. Pick out and discard as many curry leaves as you can. If you want to serve the meat off the bone, use a slotted spoon to transfer the meat to a large plate. Allow it to cool for 30 minutes, or until it is easy to touch. Wearing rubber gloves, gently pull the meat off the bones, trying to keep it whole. Return the meat to the pot and discard the bones. Gently warm the short ribs and curry on medium-high heat for 10 minutes, or until it begins to boil.

TO SERVE Place equal portions of short ribs in individual bowls and pour the curry on top (or, if you have taken the meat off the bone, spoon the meat and curry into the bowls).

SUGGESTED PAIRINGS
SPICED PICKLE-LIKE CARROTS (PAGE 32)
GOLDEN BEET, WHEAT BERRY AND SPROUTED LENTIL SALAD WITH
VIJ'S DRESSING (PAGE 133)
NAVY BEANS IN EGG AND TOMATO MASALA (PAGE 158)

MILDLY CURRIED BEEF SHORT RIBS

These short ribs are a very versatile dish that appeals to a wide range of palates. It's the recipe we make at home whenever we invite dinner guests whose kids may not enjoy spicy food. At Vij's, we spice up this recipe with more cumin and coriander and serve the Roasted Spicy Okra with Walnuts and Jelly Beans (page 94) on top. If you are not making the short ribs for kids, we recommend you try the additional spices as well as the okra. At home, we serve these short ribs with a bowl of plain white rice and some sautéed vegetables for a simple and filling meal. Ask your butcher to chop the short ribs, if you prefer.

SERVES 6 (MORE IF SERVING KIDS)
PREP & COOKING TIME: 2 ½ HOURS

IN A LARGE stockpot, heat the oil on medium-high heat for 1 minute. Add the onions and sauté for 8 minutes, or until golden. Stir in the garlic and cook for 2 to 3 minutes, or until it is light golden. Add the cumin, coriander, cayenne, turmeric, fenugreek and salt; sauté for 2 to 3 minutes. Stir in the tomatoes and cook for 2 to 3 minutes—just until they are well blended with the spices but still have their texture. Add the water and beef short ribs and stir well. Increase the heat to high and bring the mixture to a boil, then reduce the heat to low, cover and cook for 1 ½ to 2 hours, stirring occasionally. The meat is cooked when it is tender and easily falls from the bone when poked with the tip of a knife. Turn off the heat.

Using a ladle or a large spoon, skim off and discard the fat on the surface. If you cooked with bone-in short ribs and want to serve the meat off the bone, use a slotted spoon to transfer the meat to a large plate. Allow it to cool for 30 minutes, or until it is easy to touch. Wearing rubber gloves, gently pull the meat off the bones. Return the meat to the pot and discard the bones. Gently warm the short ribs and curry on medium-high heat for 10 minutes, or until it begins to boil. Remove from the heat and serve immediately.

⅓ cup cooking oil

1 ½ to 2 cups finely chopped onions (1 large)

2 tablespoons chopped garlic (6 to 7 medium cloves)

½ tablespoon ground cumin (1 ½ tablespoons, for a spicier curry)

½ tablespoon ground coriander (1 tablespoon, for a spicier curry)

1 teaspoon ground cayenne pepper (optional)

1 teaspoon turmeric

½ teaspoon ground fenugreek seeds

½ tablespoon salt

2 cups chopped fresh tomatoes (5 to 6 medium)

7 cups water

3 pounds boneless or 4 to 4 ½ pounds bone-in beef short ribs, cut into 7- to 8-ounce (if boneless) or 11- to 12-ounce (if bone-in) pieces along the bone and trimmed of extra fat

continued...

TO SERVE Divide the short ribs and curry evenly among 6 large bowls.

SUGGESTED PAIRINGS
ROASTED SPICY OKRA WITH WALNUTS AND JELLY BEANS,
WITH OR WITHOUT THE OKRA (PAGE 94)
SPROUTED LENTIL, BELL PEPPER AND CARROT SALAD (PAGE 129)
CREAMY FENUGREEK AND CUMIN POTATOES (PAGE 96)

PORK TENDERLOIN WITH HOCK IN YELLOW MUSTARD SEED AND CREAM CURRY

PORK HOCK

5 cups water

1 fresh (unsmoked) bone-in pork hock, about 2 pounds

PORK TENDERLOIN

¼ cup canola oil + more for searing

1 tablespoon salt

½ tablespoon Garam Masala (page 23) OR ground cumin

½ teaspoon ground cayenne pepper

2 ½ pounds pork tenderloin, cut into 1-inch pieces (24 pieces)

MUSTARD SEED AND CREAM CURRY

¼ to ⅓ cup cooking oil

3 tablespoons finely chopped ginger

1 tablespoon ground yellow mustard seeds

1 teaspoon ground fenugreek seeds

1 tablespoon mild ancho chili powder

1 teaspoon turmeric

1 teaspoon ground cayenne pepper

2 cups reserved pork hock stock

4 cups whipping cream

¼ cup fresh lemon juice

This braised pork is a labour of love because it takes some time to prepare, but the results are well worth the effort for a dinner party or a special occasion. On his last visit to Vancouver, Meeru's brother in-law, Gregg, who has been eating at the restaurant for fifteen years, declared this most likely the best dish he has ever eaten at Vij's.

Surprisingly, this dish is made without the three essential ingredients of Indian cooking: garlic, onions and tomatoes. What gives this curry its deep, rich flavour is the pork hock, a delicious meat that is largely overlooked in favour of more popular cuts such as pork tenderloin and baby back ribs. Jerry Gelderman of Gelderman Farms in Abbotsford told us that pork hock is as delicious as bacon if braised for the right amount of time. And he's right. Pork hock is meant for slow braising; meat prepared this way is fork-tender and the broth is very rich in flavour (even a little broth goes a long way). Don't worry about the exact yield of meat from your hock—anywhere from 6 to 9 ounces of meat is fine.

At the restaurant we serve this dish with the Millet and Bell Pepper Pilaf (page 144), but both the pork hock and its stock are very versatile. For example, you can make the Bengali-style Black Bean and Corn Curry (page 162) but use the hock meat and 2 cups of its stock in place of the whipping cream and water. Or you can do as Vikram does occasionally and add the refrigerated meat as "croutons" atop vegetarian dishes! Marinate the tenderloin while the hock is in the oven.

SERVES 6 (4 PIECES OF TENDERLOIN PER PERSON)
PREP & COOKING TIME: 4 HOURS

PORK HOCK Preheat the oven to 350°F. In a deep ovenproof pot, combine the water and pork hock, cover and bake for 3 hours (an extra half-hour will make the meat even more tender). Use tongs to transfer the hock to a large plate. Allow it to cool for 30 minutes, or until it is easy to touch.

While the hock cools, place a fine-mesh sieve over a medium bowl. Pour the pork hock stock through the sieve and set aside. (You should have about 2 cups of stock.) Discard the solids.

Wearing rubber gloves, gently pull the meat off the bones. Remove and discard the skin and visible fat. Cut the meat into bite-sized pieces and set aside. Discard the bones.

PORK TENDERLOIN In a large bowl, combine the ¼ cup of oil, salt, garam masala (or cumin) and cayenne; stir until well mixed. Add the tenderloin pieces, toss lightly to coat, and refrigerate, covered, for at least 1 hour.

MUSTARD SEED AND CREAM CURRY Heat the oil in a medium pot on medium-high heat for 30 seconds. Stir in the ginger and sauté for 1 minute. Add the mustard seeds, fenugreek, ancho chili powder, turmeric and cayenne, then stir well. Turn off the heat and allow to sit for 5 minutes.

Pour in the pork hock stock and cream, stirring well. Turn on the heat to medium, bring the curry to a boil and cook for 10 minutes, or until little orange oil bubbles glisten on top. Turn off the heat and stir in the pork hock meat and lemon juice.

FINISH CURRY AND TENDERLOIN When you are ready to serve, reheat the curry on medium heat for 10 minutes, or until it just begins to boil. Be careful not to overboil the curry or it may split.

While the curry is heating, sear the tenderloin. Pour a thin layer of canola oil into a large frying pan and heat on medium-high heat for 1 minute. Add 4 to 8 pieces of tenderloin and sear on one side for 2 minutes. Flip over and sear the second side for 2 minutes, or until medium-rare. Transfer 4 pieces of seared tenderloin to each individual serving bowl. (Don't worry about it cooling down. The hot curry will warm it right back up.) Repeat with the remaining tenderloin.

TO SERVE Pour equal portions of hock curry over the tenderloin and serve immediately.

SUGGESTED PAIRINGS
MILLET AND BELL PEPPER PILAF
(PAGE 144)
CAULIFLOWER AND POTATO IN
TOMATO MASALA (PAGE 111)
ZUCCHINI, SQUASH AND POTATO
SAUTÉ (PAGE 106)

LAMB LOIN WITH SAUTÉED BELL PEPPERS AND SUNCHOKES

¼ cup ghee or coconut oil + 2 to 3 tablespoons for searing

2 teaspoons cumin seeds

3 bell peppers, any colour, cut into large pieces

1 pound sunchokes (Jerusalem artichokes), unpeeled but scrubbed well, thinly sliced

2 teaspoons salt

½ tablespoon Garam Masala (page 23)

1 Roma or other medium tomato, chopped

12 bone-in lamb loin chops, each 3 ½ to 4 ounces, trimmed

1 to 1 ½ cups Date Chutney (page 28)

The sunchoke, also called Jerusalem artichoke, is a root vegetable that's a bit like a water chestnut and very easy to grow in British Columbia. Years ago one of our close friends, organic farmer Naty King, brought us a ten-pound bag and encouraged us to cook with them. The sunchokes grow like crazy on her farm and she is a big fan of them. Naty even made some sunchoke soup so Meeru could taste the earthy flavour. However, no matter how hard we tried to be creative, we could never figure out how to make sunchokes shine with Indian flavours. Finally we came up with this recipe, which combines a European-style presentation with fully Indian flavours. You'll need a knife and fork for this dish.

We use bone-in lamb loin chops, a cut that's less expensive than rack of lamb but just as flavourful in our view. Served with the sunchokes (or new potatoes, if you prefer) and our Date Chutney (page 28), this delicious combination comes together quickly: you sauté the vegetables and spices on high heat (with a tomato so they don't burn), then sear the meat in a bit of oil and plate the dish.

SERVES 6

PREP & COOKING TIME: 30 MINUTES

IN A LARGE frying pan, heat the ¼ cup of ghee (or coconut oil) on high heat for 1 minute. Sprinkle in the cumin seeds and allow them to sizzle for 10 to 15 seconds. Add the bell peppers, sunchokes, 1 teaspoon of the salt, garam masala and tomato; sauté, stirring regularly, for 3 to 5 minutes. Check that the sunchokes are cooked—they should have a crunchy texture but not taste raw. Turn off the heat and set aside.

Heat a heavy-bottomed or cast-iron frying pan on high heat for a few minutes. Depending on the size of your pan, you may need to cook the lamb in batches. Add 1 teaspoon ghee (or coconut oil) per 2 lamb loins and heat for 10 seconds. Place the lamb loins in the pan (you should hear a nice sizzle), reduce the heat to medium-high and sear for 4 minutes per side. To check for doneness, cut into the meat with a small knife. The centre should be pink. If it is still red, sear for 1 minute longer. Remove from the heat.

TO SERVE For a family-style presentation, arrange the lamb loin chops on a platter and sprinkle them with the remaining teaspoon of salt. Place the sautéed vegetables and the date chutney in separate bowls. For individual plates, spread 2 tablespoons of the chutney in a 6-inch circle on each dinner plate. Set 2 lamb loin chops on each plate, sprinkle with a pinch or two of the remaining salt and surround them with the sautéed vegetables. Serve immediately.

SUGGESTED PAIRINGS
LENTIL CURRY WITH SAUTÉED EGGPLANT, POTATOES AND FENNEL
(PAGE 156)
BROWN RICE AND YELLOW CHANNA DAAL PILAF (PAGE 138)
NAPA CABBAGE IN TOMATO MASALA SALAD (PAGE 59)

LAMB POPSICLES WITH GARLIC AND RICOTTA-FENUGREEK TOPPING

LAMB POPSICLES

3 pounds French-cut racks of lamb (with at least 24 ribs)

1 ½ tablespoons finely chopped garlic (4 medium cloves)

1 teaspoon salt

⅓ cup cooking oil

RICOTTA-FENUGREEK TOPPING

8 ounces full-fat ricotta cheese

1 teaspoon dried green fenugreek leaves

½ teaspoon ground cayenne pepper

1 teaspoon salt

1 bunch green onions, white and green parts, finely chopped

1 cup finely diced fresh tomatoes (2 medium)

¼ cup finely chopped cilantro (optional)

We love to cook with rack of lamb, and our signature Vij's lamb popsicles are one of our most requested recipes ever. However, this is not that dish. For private events and at home, we are always playing around with different ways to serve rack of lamb. This is the simplest version and the prettiest presentation, and it's very easy to serve as a starter (one popsicle per person) or as an entrée. We often pair these popsicles with the vegan version of the Bengali-style Curry (page 36) to make a great dinner entrée (the creamy version is too heavy with the ricotta in this recipe). If you can find some Turkish Urfa pepper, we highly recommend sprinkling some on top just before serving.

Note that the weight and the number of ribs of a rack of lamb can vary, so if the rack is meatier, you may get fewer individual popsicles, which is fine. We give the weight-to-number-of-popsicles ratio as a general guideline. If each individual popsicle is on the bigger side, we just serve fewer popsicles per person, but our guests are getting the same amount of meat. The lamb can be grilled on the barbecue or braised in the oven, depending on the season.

SERVES 6 (MAKES 24 POPSICLES)

PREP & COOKING TIME: 20 TO 30 MINUTES + 1 TO 3 HOURS TO MARINATE

LAMB POPSICLES Cut 24 chops from the racks. Place the lamb popsicles in a large bowl. Add the garlic, salt and oil and mix well until the lamb is well coated. Cover and refrigerate for 1 to 3 hours. The longer you marinate the lamb, the more "garlicky" it will become.

RICOTTA-FENUGREEK TOPPING In a bowl, combine the ricotta, fenugreek leaves, cayenne and ½ teaspoon of the salt. Set aside.

In another bowl, combine the green onions, tomatoes and ½ teaspoon of the salt. Set aside.

FINISH LAMB Preheat your barbecue or indoor grill to high or move the rack in your oven to its highest position and preheat the oven to 500°F. Mix the popsicles well one last time in the marinade.

continued...

To grill the popsicles, set them directly on the grill and cook for 2 to 3 minutes per side.

To bake the popsicles, arrange the lamb in a single layer on a large baking sheet and bake for 2 minutes per side. To check for doneness, cut into the meat with a small knife. The centre should be pink. If it is still red, bake the popsicles for 1 minute longer.

TO SERVE Arrange the popsicles on a large serving platter or on individual plates. Dollop 1 slightly heaping tablespoon of the ricotta mixture on each popsicle and then top it with a tablespoon (or slightly less) of the tomato–green onion mixture. Garnish with cilantro and serve hot.

SUGGESTED PAIRINGS
BENGALI-STYLE CURRY, VEGAN VERSION (PAGE 36)
YELLOW LENTIL CURRY WITH BLACK LENTIL MASALA (PAGE 149)
LENTIL AND BASMATI RICE PILAF WITH FRIED EGGS,
WITH OR WITHOUT THE FRIED EGGS (PAGE 140)

LAMB SHANK AND GREENS CURRY WITH "ETHIOPIAN FLAG" BASMATI RICE PILAF

This curry is heavily based on an Ethiopian curry called *gomen besiga* that Meeru's staff at the restaurant in Seattle taught her to make. Ethiopian and Indian cooking are based on many of the same spices, but they are used differently, and Ethiopian dishes are served with the traditional injera bread (made from fermented teff flour). To complete this slightly more Indian version of the lamb dish, Meeru developed a yellow, red and green pilaf—the colours of the Ethiopian flag—as an ode to this dish's origins. Made as is, this simple recipe is child friendly (if the kids eat their greens), but you will need to let them know that there are six random cloves in the curry. This dish is also easily amenable to more spices, such as cumin and coriander.

Bone-in lamb shank is the preferred meat (you may need to ask your butcher to cut the shank into smaller pieces so you can stir them more easily in your pot) and kale or collards are the preferred greens. But we have made this curry with boneless and bone-in goat meat (leg cut) and with a bit of all the leftover greens in our fridge. Ghee is a must for its flavour, as the turmeric and cumin get cooked in it and the fat from the meat. We use Indian ghee, but Ethiopians cook with *niter kibbeh*, which is clarified butter mildly spiced, commonly with green cardamom, nutmeg and cinnamon. Note that there is a lot of initial stirring in this recipe, as you don't want the turmeric or fenugreek seeds to burn and you want to cook the onions and garlic alongside the lamb shank. Prepare your rice pilaf while the curry is cooking.

Do not limit the rice pilaf to just this dish. It's a perfect accompaniment to any meat dish in this book.

SERVES 6
PREP & COOKING TIME: 1 ½ HOURS

LAMB SHANK AND GREENS CURRY Melt the ghee in a large, heavy-bottomed pot on high heat. Add the onions and sauté for 2 to 3 minutes, then reduce the heat to medium-high and add the lamb. Continue to stir and cook for 10 minutes. The meat will release some fat and the onions will begin to sweat and appear more translucent. If the bottom of your pot is turning dark brown, either reduce the heat or add 1 tablespoon of ghee.

LAMB SHANK AND GREENS CURRY

¼ to ⅓ cup ghee

3 cups chopped onions (3 to 4 medium)

3 pounds lamb shank, cut into 3 to 4 pieces

3 tablespoons chopped garlic (9 to 10 medium cloves)

1 teaspoon turmeric

1 teaspoon ground fenugreek seeds (optional)

¾ cup chopped tomatoes (1 medium)

6 whole cloves

1 tablespoon ground cumin

1 teaspoon salt

6 cups water

3 bunches collards or kale, stems discarded, roughly chopped

ETHIOPIAN FLAG RICE PILAF

1 ½ cups Basmati rice

2 ¾ cups water

1 tablespoon + 1 teaspoon cooking oil

1 teaspoon turmeric

¼ teaspoon asafoetida (optional)

2 teaspoons salt

1 green bell pepper, cut into 1-inch pieces

1 red bell pepper, cut into 1-inch pieces

7 to 9 ounces Paneer (page 38), cubed (optional)

continued...

Stir in the garlic and cook, stirring, for 5 minutes. Add the turmeric and fenugreek, stir well and cook for 2 minutes. Stir in the tomatoes, cloves, cumin and salt. (The tomatoes prevent the cumin from sticking too much to the pot.) Continue to stir and cook for 3 minutes. Add the water and stir some more, then increase the heat to high and bring the curry to a boil. Reduce the heat to low, cover and cook for 45 minutes.

After 45 minutes, stir in the greens. Cover and cook for 20 to 30 minutes, or until the lamb begins to come off the bones. Remove from the heat. If you want to serve the meat off the bone, use tongs to transfer the meat to a bowl and allow it to cool for 30 minutes. Wearing rubber gloves, gently pull the meat off the bones. Return the meat to the pot and discard the bones.

ETHIOPIAN FLAG RICE PILAF Place the rice in a medium bowl, wash it well under cold water and drain. Repeat the washing and draining once more. Combine the rice with the 2 ¾ cups water in a pot and allow it to soak for 30 minutes. Turn on the heat to high, add the 1 teaspoon of oil and bring the rice to a boil. Reduce the heat to a simmer, cover and cook the rice for 15 minutes. Turn off the heat and allow to sit, covered, for 5 minutes.

While the rice is cooking, pour the 1 tablespoon of oil into a frying pan just large enough to hold the bell peppers in a single layer (you want to use as little oil as possible but still need to coat the spices). Place the pan on medium-high heat for 1 minute. Add the turmeric and asafoetida, stir and cook for 1 minute. The turmeric will become a darker orange. Add the salt and the bell peppers, stir well and sauté for 5 minutes, or until the bell peppers are cooked but still al dente. Stir in the paneer (if using).

To finish the pilaf, gently stir the bell pepper mixture into the cooked rice. Stir some rice into the frying pan to absorb all of the spices, then return that savoury rice to the pilaf and stir it in.

TO SERVE Divide the rice pilaf among 6 large bowls and top with lots of the lamb curry.

SUGGESTED PAIRINGS
CUCUMBER RAITA (PAGE 33)
SPICED PUMPKINS SEEDS (PAGE 40)
NAPA CABBAGE IN TOMATO MASALA
SALAD (PAGE 59)

CONVERSION CHART

WEIGHT

IMPERIAL	METRIC
1 oz	28 g
2 oz	55 g
3 oz	85 g
4 oz (¼ lb)	115 g
5 oz	140 g
6 oz	170 g
7 oz	200 g
8 oz (½ lb)	225 g
9 oz	250 g
10 oz	285 g
11 oz (⅔ lb)	300 g
12 oz (¾ lb)	340 g
13 oz	365 g
14 oz	400 g
15 oz	425 g
16 oz (1 lb)	450 g
2 lb	900 g
2 ½ lb	1.125 kg
3 lb	1.35 kg
3 ½ lb	1.6 kg
4 lb	1.8 kg
4 ½ lb	2 kg

VOLUME

IMPERIAL	METRIC
⅛ tsp	0.5 mL
¼ tsp	1 mL
½ tsp	2 mL
¾ tsp	4 mL
1 tsp	5 mL
2 tsp	10 mL
1 Tbsp	15 mL
1½ Tbsp	22 mL
2 Tbsp	30 mL
¼ cup	60 mL
⅓ cup	75 mL
½ cup	125 mL
⅔ cup	150 mL
¾ cup	175 mL
1 cup	250 mL
2 cups	500 mL
3 cups	750 mL
4 cups	1L

TEMPERATURE

IMPERIAL	METRIC
250°F	120°C
275°F	140°C
300°F	150°C
325°F	160°C
350°F	180°C
375°F	190°C
400°F	200°C
425°F	220°C
450°F	230°C
475°F	240°C
500°F	260°C

INDEX